THE
TRAP

THE IMAGE TRAP

A NOVEL BY LISA DUNCAN

BOOKCRAFT
Salt Lake City, Utah

All characters in this book are fictitious,
and any resemblance to actual persons,
living or dead, is purely coincidental.

Library of Congress Catalog Card Number: 91-72457

ISBN 0-88494-795-5

First Printing, 1991

Printed in the United States of America

_____ One

Upstairs in her bedroom, Joanne peered through a crack in the venetian blind as her mother's car came up the driveway. This was a black day. Despite all Joanne's objections, her cousin Novi Kosnowski was arriving.

Not that Joanne had anything specific against her cousin. She hadn't even seen Novi for eight years – when they were both nine years old Novi's family had moved to a city in another province. So really, Joanne wasn't even sure what to expect. But she had her suspicions. She remembered what Novi had been like when they were nine, and if Novi now was even remotely like what she had been then, Joanne was in trouble.

Before the other family's move, the two girls had been forced together practically from birth – they were born in the same year and only two months apart – and while they were still on all fours and in diapers this arrangement had worked well. The older they grew, however, the more their incompatibility became apparent. Novi always wanted to dress up in strange costumes, or do puppet shows, or play detectives or pirates. Joanne just wanted to play Barbies, or sit at the kitchen table and color. And when they got their bikes out in the summer Novi would always race ahead and would then

1

have to circle back again and again because Joanne liked to pedal at a nice, easy pace. Basically, it seemed that Novi and Joanne wanted different things from life.

So when they started school and were put in different grade one classes, they made their own friends and chose new playmates for their after-school games. And once this happened it became clear that it had only been for the sake of the girls that their mothers had stayed in close contact, and soon the families drifted apart. In fact, in the year before the Kosnowskis moved away from the Clarke's area, the sisters, Novi's and Joanne's moms saw each other only three times.

While all this was going on Joanne sensed that there were problems and tensions in the other family that she was too young to understand, but once the Kosnowskis were gone she never really thought to ask her mother what they were. Her mother didn't talk about her sister, and as far as Joanne knew, no effort had been made to stay in touch with the Kosnowskis, who now lived a long day's drive away. It turned out, though, that Trish Clarke had made infrequent but regular attempts to maintain contact with her sister, as Joanne found out two weeks before Christmas when her mother announced that Novi was coming to live with them.

This news suddenly forced her cousin back into Joanne's mind, and the more she thought about Novi's impending arrival the more it bothered her. Memories of the time when she and Novi had still played together crept back in. She could still remember the time when Novi had somehow talked her into sitting on the front lawn and pounding two big pots with wooden spoons while Novi recited some poetry she had written. Kids had stopped and laughed, and cars had slowed for the spectacle. Novi had loved the attention, but Joanne had just felt stupid.

So when Joanne and her mother were together making shortbread cookies in the kitchen a few days before Christmas, about a week before Novi was scheduled to arrive, Joanne had to speak her mind.

"Mom, can't Novi go stay with Uncle Steve?"

"That's charitable of you," her mother said.

"What's going on? Why does she have to come here? I mean, I have enough problems already. I don't need a weird cousin around to complicate things."

"Honestly, Joanne," her mother scolded. "How do you know she's weird? And even if she is, what difference does it make? She's coming, and you'd better be nice to her."

"And I have no say in the matter?"

"Nope." Her mother smudged cookie dough on the end of Joanne's nose, but Joanne refused to be amused.

And now the fateful day had arrived. Watching from her bedroom window, Joanne could see first the top of her mother's head as she got out of the car, then the top of her cousin's head. Joanne shrieked in horror. "White hair!" she yelled. Her worst fears were being realized. Novi had punk-white hair spiking out of her head—and she was about to enter the house.

Joanne heard the front door open and close.

"Joanne," her mother called up to her.

She expects me to go downstairs and be cheerful and friendly to my white-haired cousin, Joanne thought. "White hair, white hair," she muttered to herself in disbelief. It was almost too much to bear.

"Joanne!"

Joanne knew that the longer she waited the more awkward things would be, so she decided to just get it over with as quickly as possible. *One brief moment of pain,* she thought, *and then I can hide in my room until she goes back home.* Joanne fixed a smile on her face and went downstairs.

Her smile disappeared when she reached the front entranceway and got a good look at her cousin. Pointy black boots adorned with silver buckles; black baggy pants; a big black shirt; an oversized men's blazer—also black; black leather gloves; and, of course, the hair, shockingly white,

3

with short sides, sticking up messily on top. Joanne let her eyes travel up and down over the bundle of black that was her cousin Novi. *What on earth was Aunt Elaine thinking when she named this girl Novi?* Joanne thought. *What kind of person did she expect her to become? Talk about self-fulfilling prophecy.*

After looking Novi over thoroughly, Joanne finally couldn't help but let her eyes rest on the reddest lipstick she had ever seen. She stood there in the front hallway transfixed, hypnotized into shock and terror by Novi's lips.

Her mother cleared her throat threateningly. "Joanne, you remember Novi."

"Hello," Joanne said. She had an incredible urge to ask Novi who had died.

"Hi," Novi said.

Silence.

"Well, it was nice . . . seeing you," Joanne said, and she turned away, hoping to escape.

Trish Clarke cleared her throat again. "Why don't you help Novi with her things and show her to her room, Joanne."

Joanne was trapped. "Yes, mother," she muttered. In silence she helped Novi unload the car. In silence she led her upstairs.

Joanne had hoped to show Novi her room and leave it at that. Actually, she had hoped that after the initial introductory disaster she would be able to ignore her cousin completely and try to forget that she existed. After all, it was obvious that Joanne couldn't be seen in public with her. She wasn't sure how she would explain Novi to her friends, but she would have to think of something: perhaps that Novi was a runaway who had just showed up one day and was kindly taken in by the Clarkes; or maybe, that she was a ward of the province, a delinquent who chose Joanne's family rather than a juvenile detention center. That sounded convincing.

Of course, Joanne could never really do this, no matter how much she wanted to. She did have occasional pangs of conscience, and besides that her mother would never allow it. As it was, she called Joanne into the kitchen while Novi unpacked.

"Sit!" Trish commanded. Joanne sat.

Her mother glared at her for a moment from across the table. "Well," she began, "that was quite the gracious welcome you gave our guest, Joanne."

Joanne stared at a bread crumb on the table in front of her.

"Do you honestly think Novi didn't notice the way you looked at her?"

"But, Mom . . ."

"Listen, honey." Her mother's voice softened. "I know she looks a little bit . . . well, unconventional, but it's a hard time for her, okay? Please make an effort, Jo."

Joanne said nothing.

"Why don't you go see if she needs any help unpacking."

Joanne grasped desperately for something to say. "You're in grade twelve, right?"

"Yep," Novi replied.

"So, I guess you'll be graduating here?"

"Unless I flunk."

Joanne laughed half-heartedly.

There was another awkward pause. Joanne leaned against the wall, shocked anew at each strange piece of clothing Novi hung in the closet.

"Did your mom tell you why I was coming?" Novi suddenly asked.

Joanne was caught off guard. She had been trying to figure out what the mass of orange fabric was that Novi had just pulled from her suitcase. "What?"

"Did your mom explain why I was coming to stay here?"

"Uh . . . well, sort of. She just said your family was having a few problems. And that if you wanted to talk about it, well, you would." Joanne wasn't sure she wanted to hear any of the sordid details of her cousin's life. It seemed to her that if Novi were to confide in her, at that moment some sort of commitment would be made, some kind of doorway would be opened to the possibility of friendship. Joanne wanted none of it. Besides that, she had been formulating her own ideas about why Novi had been thrust upon her. Before she had arrived, Joanne had imagined some minor problems at school or at home, but having seen Novi she was sure it was much worse than that. Armed robbery perhaps. Or maybe she was a drug addict.

"Well, my parents just separated," Novi began. "Actually, my dad ran off. We don't know where he went. I guess my mom kind of fell apart, so she asked your mom to take me off her hands for a while."

"Oh." It was all Joanne could think of to say. She felt like a real schmuck now. "Are you . . . are you okay?" she stammered.

Novi shrugged. "I only told you so that you'd know why I'm here. You have a right to know why you have this new intruder in your house."

Joanne stopped staring at the floor and looked up at Novi. *Have I been that obvious?* she wondered, all the while knowing that she had been.

But Novi smiled at her. "Cousin, dear," she said, "I have a serious question to ask you. Where's the bathroom?"

When Larry Clarke came home from work and saw Novi, he tried his best to act nonchalant. When Joanne's twelve-year-old brother, Scott, got home from the friend's house where he had spent the day, he didn't try at all.

"You probably don't remember Novi," his mother said to him.

"Yeah, I would have remembered you," Scott said as he looked Novi up and down. "Wow!"

And when the family sat down for supper, things were strangely quiet. There was a lot of throat clearing and chair shifting, and occasionally one of the parents made a valiant effort to converse, but their questions were met with curt, one-syllable answers, and silence always flooded back in. Joanne just couldn't find the strength to talk.

Finally Larry Clarke spoke up. "So, Novi. How was the trip here?"

"Oh, it was fine. Except this woman sat beside me on the bus from the city, and the whole way she snapped her gum and yelled at me in this loud voice about her psychic niece. She said the kid could foresee the future. Apparently she always correctly guessed whether new babies in their family would be boys or girls." Novi stopped. The Clarkes looked at her as if they had just heard a gun shot. Then they remembered to smile, but such an extended monologue left them more speechless than ever. Finally Scott spoke.

"Hey, Novi. What's with the clothes? Who died?"

Joanne couldn't help laughing. Novi laughed too. But Joanne could tell by the look on her mother's face that Scott was in trouble. The meal was finished in tense silence.

_____ Two

Joanne sat cross-legged on her bed and considered the disastrous turn her life had taken. The room was dark except for the light from the street lamp outside her window. She felt at a complete loss to know what to do. Novi was now a reality—a more horrifying reality than she had imagined possible. The future played out in Joanne's mind like her worst nightmare: Novi comes to school with Joanne and meets Joanne's friends, who ruthlessly mock and taunt them both and leave Joanne shunned and abandoned in a cold, empty hallway. Beyond that Joanne's imagination halted, unwilling to contemplate any further horrors.

So Joanne knew what she had to do. It might mean trouble at home, but she would risk it. Novi seemed nice enough, as Joanne had painfully noted when the family had played Monopoly after dinner that evening. Novi had been relaxed and friendly, and when Joanne, in the midst of cash-flow problems, had landed on Novi's Hotel Boardwalk, Novi had let Joanne stay free. And Novi was pretty funny too. She had zapped Scott with a couple of good-natured zingers, and that always got points with Joanne. _Okay, so she's nice,_ Joanne said to herself, _but I will not let myself feel bad. I will not let myself like her. She's too weird. I know exactly what_ *my friends will think of her. I can't deny that she's my cousin, but I can make sure we're never seen together. If I don't throw Novi to the wolves, it'll be me that gets eaten. Besides, she's leaving in a few months, and it doesn't make any sense to risk all my friends for a girl I barely know and will probably never see again after she goes.*

Joanne was willing to go through this intricate series of rationalizations because she knew all too well how precarious her position was in the social world of her school. True, she was considered to be a member of the élite group, but to those in the know it was obvious that Joanne stood dangerously on the fringe. Novi's presence alone was a threat, but if they became friends Joanne could be sent hurtling into social oblivion.

I don't care what my mother does, Joanne decided. *She can't make me be friends with Novi. Novi is on her own.*

With that Joanne got into bed, pulled her quilt up to her chin, and tried to sleep.

Novi sat cross-legged on her bed writing in the coil notebook that she used as a journal.

thursday january 2

well, i've really arrived now. what a day. flight from winnipeg, bus from edmonton, and now here i am in my new room in the clarke house. i can't quite believe it. everything is changing so fast. anyway, as for my temporary new family, they met me with various degrees of shock. aunt trish and uncle larry are very nice and really tried to be cool. scott is a basic 12 year old kid. i think i'll be an asset to him, kind of like a black eye he can show off. every 12 year old likes a little negative attention. then there's joanne. if i recall correctly, joanne was uptight as a little kid, and obviously that hasn't changed. when she first saw me she just about fainted. i swear, i thought she was going to scream or something. she gave me the once over with this look of horror on her face. after that she tried to be nice, even though she only did it because she got a lecture from her mom. i can just imagine what's going on in her head: "what are my friends going to think?" well, she doesn't have to worry. i'll leave her alone. i understand her situation.

it's kind of too bad though. i like the girl. and i don't exactly have an abundance of social contacts in this town.

one nice thing today was playing monopoly with the whole family, everyone just enjoying each other's company, which is a slightly foreign experience for me. never see that family unity stuff at my house. obviously.

Novi reread the entry, then added a final note.

i miss my dad.

Three

Joanne and Novi were in the family room when Trish strode in. Joanne was doing some math homework at the coffee table and Novi was draped in the big easy chair reading.

"I've got a great idea, Jo," her mother said. "Why don't you take Novi skating with you tonight. You can introduce her to your friends."

Oh, perfect, Mom, Joanne thought. *That's exactly what I've been dying to do.* "Uh . . . it probably won't be much fun." She quickly glanced at Novi. "I'm sure Novi'd hate it."

"Nonsense," her mother insisted. "You like skating, don't you, Novi?"

Novi looked at Joanne, who was chewing nervously at her bottom lip. Novi had no desire to go where she was obviously not wanted. "Oh, it's impossible. Doctor's orders. I have bad ankles." Trish laughed. "Besides, I don't have any skates."

But Trish persisted. "I'm sure we can find you some skates. Mine will probably fit you."

Joanne and Novi argued but could not prevail, and at seven o'clock they were on their way to the rink.

"Are you sure your friends won't mind my coming?" Novi asked as they drove.

13

Joanne shook her head. She couldn't speak. Her stomach was churning, and despite the cold January air beads of sweat were gathering on her forehead. *This is it,* she thought. *This night marks the end of my life. From now on, I am an outcast.*

As soon as Joanne thought this, though, a cry of protest rose up from a small place in the back of her mind; a tiny island to which she had banished everything that stood in the way of the choices she had made, the way she had decided to live. For just a moment, as she drove towards the skating rink where she knew her friends were all gathered, a shadow passed across her mind, a hint of the wrongness of everything she was doing, a questioning shadow that asked, Is this happiness? Is this how you want your life to go? Is this how you want to feel? What are you giving up, and what are you getting for it?

Joanne glanced over at Novi, who was sitting beside her in the car with her pointy black boots and her pointy white hair. Seeing her as she knew her friends would see her, Joanne shuddered. The brief moment of protest passed, along with the shadow on her mind. Joanne refused to acknowledge them.

The gang were already in the process of putting on their skates when Joanne and Novi walked into the rink-side shack. Everyone smiled and shouted hello, but when they realized that Novi was with Joanne their expressions changed.

"Hi everyone," Joanne said, trying to act casual. Joanne's friends stared at Novi. For a moment nobody moved.

Joanne gulped. "Uh . . . this is my cousin Novi. She's staying with us for a while. Novi, this is Buffy, Doug, Cam, Jill, and Todd." They nodded as their names were called, making no attempt to hide their disapproval. *So that's how I looked when I first saw Novi,* Joanne thought. She wasn't very pleased with herself or with her friends. Everyone solemnly waited while she and Novi put on their skates.

Once outside, things loosened up a bit. The gang played screaming games of Crack the Whip and practiced figure skating moves. They took each other on in speed skating races, and flung themselves into the snow banks that surrounded the rink. A cloud of conspiracy hung over them, however, an unspoken resolve not to let Novi into their circle. They weren't mean to her, but they weren't nice, either. Novi could feel it, and so could Joanne.

While everyone skated around, showing off to each other, Buffy, the center of this circle of friends, took Joanne's arm and pulled her away from the others. Joanne knew what was coming.

"Your cousin has an interesting sense of style," Buffy said.

"Yes." *Out with it, Buffy,* Joanne thought.

"Look, Jo. I know you had no choice in having your cousin stay with you. All I have to say is, be careful who you associate with."

"You sound like my mother," Joanne said, trying to act nonchalant. Buffy laughed, and the two girls skated back to the others. Buffy squeezed Joanne's arm before she let it go. Joanne felt sick.

Novi had been watching this little exchange, and when Joanne skated back they looked at each other. From the expression on Joanne's face, Novi knew what had been said.

Cam Wilson had been watching too. So far he had been going along with the gang's little game, but after watching Buffy in action — as Alexis Carrington-like as ever — he couldn't do it anymore. *Being popular is one thing,* he thought; *being a jerk is another.* He skated over to Novi.

"Hi," he said apologetically. "I'm Cam, in case you forgot."

Rather shocked that one of the gang was speaking to her, Novi eyed Cam with suspicion. She was having a hard time in suppressing her resentment toward Joanne's smug friends; in fact, she wanted to be snide and snarling and to match

15

their quiet cruelty with sarcasm. But she controlled herself: she had tried that response before and it had never got her anywhere.

"Are you a Mormon?" Cam asked.

Novi shook her head.

"Oh, well, I just wondered, since Joanne's family is. Are you going to church with them on Sunday?"

"I doubt it." Novi liked the Clarkes, but she had no desire to go to church with them.

"Oh, come on. You'd love it. We could sit togehter in Sunday School."

Novi searched Cam's face but could find no trace of sarcasm or deception. *He must be sincere,* she thought, so she smiled and played along. "Aren't you being a little forward, young man? I mean, I have standards. I don't just go to Sunday School with *anyone.*"

"I'm really sorry, Miss. Let me make it up to you." Cam plopped a handful of snow on Novi's head. Novi then shoved Cam into a snowbank. They both laughed. Novi's desire to snarl at Joanne's friends was dissipating.

After everyone's toes had begun to freeze and their ankles had begun to wobble, the group left the rink and went to Jill's house, where they sat around in the basement warming their hands on their mugs of hot chocolate, talking about Christmas, playing pool, and just relaxing. Novi was much more at ease knowing that she had at least one ally in Cam. Joanne, however, felt worse than ever. She knew that Buffy's "advice" boiled down to an ultimatum: Novi or the gang. She couldn't have it both ways. She knew what the right choice was, but she also knew how much she wanted to keep her friends. *Why should I have to choose? It's not fair.* Joanne was thinking this when Cam came up to her.

"I really like your cousin, Jo."

"Yeah. She's okay." It was this fact that bothered Joanne. If Novi had been less okay, less likeable, everything would have been easier.

"We weren't very nice to her tonight. I feel bad about that. I don't know why people have to be such jerks." Cam figured Joanne would automatically agree with him, since they both had the same ideas about right and wrong. Joanne just nodded.

The little gathering only lasted about an hour. Doug, Todd, and Cam drove home together in Todd's car.

"Hey, Cam." Doug said, as they backed out of Jill's driveway. "Getting kind of friendly with the punker, aren't you?"

"Ha, ha." Cam didn't really want to get into this.

"Great hair," Todd said.

"Not nearly as great as those boots," Doug said. "Talk about lethal weapons."

"Nice legs, shame about the hair." Doug and Todd laughed loudly.

Cam was getting angry. *Why do these guys feel they have to act this way?* he wondered. "Why don't you guys just shut up."

"Ooh! Now he's sticking up for her."

"You guys make me sick. It takes a lot of brains to make fun of someone's hair, doesn't it?"

Doug and Todd looked at each other and were silent for the rest of the ride. When they got to Cam's house Todd slammed on the brakes and fishtailed the car to a stop.

"Here's where you get off, Cameron," Doug said sarcastically.

"Later, buddy," Todd sneered.

As Todd and Doug sped away, Cam realized he was putting a lighted match to his social bridges. *This had better be worth it,* he thought.

Joanne and Novi drove home in silence. Novi looked out of the window at the town that years ago had been her home. The fact that it was her home again depressed her, as much for the problems that had brought her here as for the problems that were developing now that she had arrived. Novi felt bad that she was to blame for Joanne's emotional turmoil, that her presence had forced Joanne into the situation she was now in. After all, although Novi was used to being on the outside of things – as it was a territory she had to some extent chosen and had had years to get used to – Novi realized it was unfair that Joanne should be banished to that territory, and for that banishment, if it was to come, she was sorry.

When they arrived home and pulled into the driveway, Novi turned to Joanne and started to speak.

"Joanne, I think I know what Buffy said to you. You have to choose between me and them, right?"

Joanne was silent. She pressed the automatic garage door opener, drove into the garage, then stared straight ahead, unable to meet Novi's eyes. The garage door hummed shut behind them.

"You don't owe me anything," Novi continued, "and I have no right to expect anything, so don't worry about it. I mean, personally I don't think the way I look is a big deal. It seems natural to me, but I know it's not for everyone. That's okay."

Joanne shut off the engine and then turned to Novi. "I don't understand."

"I'm saying that I won't be hurt if you choose your friends. Don't worry about me."

"My mom would kill me."

"Your mom doesn't have to know."

_____ Four

Except for Larry, who had gone to work earlier that morning, all the Clarke family were in the kitchen. Trish was washing the dishes, Joanne was drying them, and Scott was doing his best to annoy his mom and his sister by swatting them with the broom he was supposed to be sweeping with.

"Stop it, Scott," his mother laughed.

"How did last night go, hon?" Trish asked Joanne.

"Fine," Joanne replied. She was feeling particularly gloomy today. She resented Novi's existence, and especially Novi's kindness. It just made her feel guilty.

"Did everything go all right with Novi?"

"They think she's weird, Mom."

"And you're not?" Scott blurted out. Joanne told her brother to shut up.

"Well, so what if she's a little different?"

"You don't know my friends," Joanne muttered.

Her mother looked at Joanne, who was sullenly drying the dishes. "Jo, I know this is hard, but even if your friends don't accept Novi, you have to."

"Why?"

"I'm not even going to answer that. You know why. They weren't mean to her, were they?"

"Well, not openly. Cam was nice to her."

"That's good," Trish said as she washed the last cereal bowl. "Hopefully you two have a different perspective on things."

Joanne rolled her eyes. The thought came that it would be so much easier if she *didn't* have a different perspective.

"I'm sorry you've been put in this position, Jo."

"Yeah, I'm sorry too."

"I like Novi's hair," Scott said as he swatted Joanne with the broom.

"You would!" Joanne said.

That evening after dinner, Larry and Trish sat together in the living room reading. Scott was at the hockey practice and Novi and Joanne were in their respective rooms.

Suddenly Larry put down his book. "Honey, what's that smell?"

His wife looked up from her book and sniffed.

"Does it smell like smoke to you?" Larry asked.

They looked at each other, frowning. "Novi," they said in unison. They put down their books and trudged upstairs.

Knock, knock, knock.

"Who is it?" Novi called out from inside her room.

"It's Trish and Larry. Can we talk to you?"

"Uh . . . just a sec." Novi was panicking, frantically trying to shove smoke out of her open window. After positioning herself on the bed, she called out "Come in."

"Hi," said the couple as they entered.

"Hi," said Novi.

There followed an uncomfortable moment of silence. Trish looked at Larry and nodded to him, so he began.

"Uh, Novi, were you smoking?"

For a minute Novi considered lying, but the evidence against her was too strong. Despite her previous frantic efforts it floated around her head—a haze of smoke. "Yes," she answered meekly.

"Oh," said the couple, unsure of what to say next.

"I started smoking in grade nine," Novi explained. "I

don't know, I always thought it was kind of sophisticated. Like Bette Davis or something."

"I always thought it caused cancer," Trish said.

"Yeah, I guess so. But I'm nervous, you know? So I just took up smoking instead of biting my nails. I'd probably take up eating and gain fifty pounds if I ever quit."

Larry cleared his throat. *Oh no,* Novi thought. *Here comes something serious.*

"Uh . . . Novi, since you're going to be living here for a while, I guess we should lay down some ground rules for you. You know, house rules. The same ones we've given Scott and Joanne."

Novi made a pained face. The Clarkes laughed, and the situation was eased considerably. Trish was noticing that Novi had a talent for this.

"I guess that's fair," Novi said. "Shoot."

"Okay," Larry began, "first of all, we obey the Word of Wisdom in our house."

"The word of what?"

"The Word of Wisdom. It's part of our religion. We don't drink alcohol or tea or coffee, or smoke. No drugs, either. Basically, it's a good health plan."

"Does this mean you want me to quit smoking?" Novi asked, this time with a genuine look of pain on her face.

"Well, don't you think it would be good for you? You're awfully young to be chained to a habit like that," Trish pointed out.

"I guess so," Novi admitted reluctantly. "Can I at least ease out of it?"

"No smoking in the house," Larry said, trying to be diplomatic.

Novi nodded.

"Next, no swearing in the house."

"What if I think a swear word?" Novi asked.

"We don't really have control over that," Trish laughed.

"Curfew is midnight, and no boys in your bedroom." *Midnight,* Novi was thinking. *Midnight? What is this, reform school?* She was used to a less restricted lifestyle. She kept her mouth closed, though.

"We'd also like it if you'd come to church with us on Sundays."

"What?"

"We want you to come to church with us."

"Wait a minute," Novi said, sitting up straight. "I can live with those other rules, even if they are just a tiny bit strict. But why should I have to go to your church? I mean, I'm just not a religious person. I won't do anything bad while you're gone, if that's what you're worried about."

"No, that's not it. We want you to be a part of our family. And on Sundays that's what our family does. Oh, and on Mondays we try to have something called family home evening together. We usually have some kind of lesson or activity."

Novi groaned. She enjoyed the Clarkes, but not that much. *What's with this family unity stuff?* she thought. Its original novelty was quickly wearing off.

"You seem like the kind of person who is open to new experience. Why don't you just try it?" Trish coaxed.

Novi had to give her aunt credit for her argument. Novi did pride herself on her open-mindedness. Even so, she didn't like the idea of religion being shoved at her. "I don't have anything to wear to church."

"Oh, that's no problem. You can borrow something of Jo's until we get you some Sunday clothes."

Novi tried but couldn't think of any more excuses why she couldn't go to church. *I guess it can't hurt,* she thought grudgingly. "Anything else?"

"No, that's it," Larry said. "It's not too bad, is it?"

"Not too bad?" Novi asked incredulously. "Not too bad? Not too bad if you're a nun, maybe."

Her uncle and aunt laughed. "Novi, we also want you to know that if you need anything you can come to us. You're completely welcome here. If you need to talk, if you need to buy something for school, anything, you can come to us, okay?''

"Yeah, okay. Sorry about the smoke."

"Oh, one more thing," Larry said. "How does fifteen dollars a week for allowance sound? It's not much, but I'm just a lowly country lawyer."

"No," Novi insisted. She felt bad enough taking food and shelter from them. "You don't have to give me an allowance."

"But if we want to, will you please take it?" Trish asked.

Novi smiled. Larry and Trish both kissed Novi on the cheek, then left the room, closing the door behind them.

"Did I do okay?" Larry asked.

"You did fine."

"I had to force myself not to look at her hair."

Trish laughed. "I kind of like it, you know. What do you think?" she said, fingering her hair. "Do you think it would suit me?"

"I dare you," he said. Together they walked downstairs, laughing and feeling relieved.

The phone rang just as Scott burst in the back door from hockey practice. He ran to the kitchen and answered it.

"Joanne!" he screamed. "Telephone!" Joanne came downstairs from her room, where she had been unsuccessfully trying to figure out her life.

Scott teased her, yanking the phone away each time she reached for it. "Give it to me, you loser," Joanne shouted at him. Finally he did.

"Hello?"

"Hi Jo."

"Oh. Hi Jill," Joanne said unenthusiastically.

"I know what you mean," Jill said. "This cousin thing is pretty bad, eh? I guess Buffy told you where she stands. What are you going to do about it?"

"I don't know why we let Buffy boss us around. Who made her the minister of social acceptance anyway?"

"She did," Jill said. "And we did." Jill and Joanne had a secret resentment toward Buffy, but they stuck around anyway. They knew that you don't just leave your high school gang. Besides that, there was nowhere else to go.

"Novi is pretty weird, though," Jill said.

"I don't know what the big deal is," Joanne snapped. "Just because her hair is white. So what?"

"Hey, don't yell at me, Joanne. You weren't exactly raving about her last night."

"Sorry, Jill." *Jill's right,* Joanne thought. *I'm a hypocrite if I start defending Novi now. I'm a hypocrite anyway.* "Well," she said, "it's not going to be so bad. Novi kind of said she'd keep her distance. She understands my position."

"Oh, that's good. I mean, she can't really expect anything can she?"

"Yeah, well . . . look, I've got to go."

The girls said good-bye. Joanne hung up and flopped down at the kitchen table. She could feel disgust rising within her; disgust for Jill's attitude, and especially for her own. For an instant she could see her own face, looking the way her friends had looked when they first saw Novi, and she was shocked at the ugliness of its expression. She quickly blinked the picture away and left the kitchen.

Novi was in her room. She didn't feel comfortable enough to just roam around the house, since this was only her third day at the Clarkes', so for now she kept to herself. She sat at the little desk in the corner, writing in her journal.

saturday january 4

well, i've been here 2 days and i'm still alive. not without battle scars however. yesterday i went skating with joanne and her friends. what a farce. it amazes me how people can be in the same room with you, within

24

inches of you, and still pretend that you don't exist. it was an interesting experience not existing for an evening though. joanne was utterly uncomfortable the whole night. torn between being nice to me—which her friends wouldn't have liked too much—or joining in with her friends. i tried to relieve her anguish by telling her to forget about me. i don't want the poor girl to have a breakdown. there was one nice boy though. he actually talked to me. how brave.

oh yes. trish and larry set down the law tonight. NO SMOKING! MIDNIGHT CURFEW! and to top it all off, i have to go to church with them on sundays!

well, i didn't make a fuss about the smoking. i guess if i'm honest about it, i don't enjoy it that much. it's more like a nervous habit. something to do with my hands. this is not to say that it will be easy to quit. i'll start biting my nails again and turn into a blimp. as for the curfew, the more i think about it, the more i realize that there's no where in this town that's even open after midnight. i think i'll be spending most of my nights in this little room, alone. social possibilities don't look too promising here.

as for this church thing, i'm a little worried. oh mom, let me come home. i try to be a positive person but, no friends, no social life, no nervous habits? the future is looking very bleak. i wonder how mom is anyway? i wonder how dad is? or where he is for that matter. i miss them both, despite everything. i've been trying to figure out just what went on, but i can't. i wonder if dad even considered me when he left. i wish i could talk to him so he could explain.

it's late. church tomorrow. school on monday. arghh!! sure i'm brave. sure i'm an individual and i can stand on my own. still, facing masses of indifferent, or worse, hostile people, isn't my idea of fun.

maybe dad will call me or something.

_____ _Five_

Novi decided to make the most of going to church. _Why not make a game of it?_ she thought. _Why not try to shock all those church-going folks?_ So she got dressed.

She borrowed a narrow, mid-calf-length black skirt from Joanne, wore black tights under it, and put on a pair of the pointiest black flats she owned. On top she wore a very baggy black turtleneck sweater. She added her favorite necklace—a large African voodoo charm dangling from a leather string —and huge hoop earrings. Her white hair was teased to new heights and her lips were a dark plum color—almost purple.

Novi looked at herself in the full-length mirror in her room. "Groovy," she said, smiling.

When the Clarkes walked into the chapel, it seemed that the entire congregation turned to look at them in a gradually spreading wave of curiosity. Novi grinned. Sheepishly, Larry and Trish looked for a place to sit. Scott beamed, delighted to be associated with his bizarre cousin. Joanne stared at her shoes, quickly sinking into new depths of despair and humiliation.

As soon as Cam Wilson saw Novi, he smiled. He couldn't help respecting her for her outright defiance of everything. He was anxious for sacrament meeting to end so that he could talk to her. Ever since the party, he had been thinking about Novi. He wasn't in exactly the same position as Joanne, but he knew that he had to make a choice; he couldn't be friends with Novi and with the gang.

So he had been examining his own priorities. *Why do I hang around with Doug and Todd?* he had asked himself. *They can be such pigs sometimes. Am I really happy with them, or are they just a habit? Why do I tolerate Buffy's little cruelties, and even join in on them?* Like Joanne, Cam was disgusted with himself. *If I'm going to be able to live with myself,* he thought, *things have got to change.* And Cam felt thankful to Novi for his new resolve.

Cam had been thinking about Novi so much that he had mentioned her to his mother. "She sounds very interesting," she had said. But when Cam announced his momentous decision to make a break from the gang, she was worried.

"Why take up with this new girl when you have such nice friends already?"

"I didn't say I was taking up with her, Mom. She just makes me think about things. And my friends aren't that nice."

"Sure they are. I've met all your friends, and they're nice kids."

Obviously Cam didn't tell his mother some of the things he and the gang did at school—the cruelties, the teasing, the backbiting. She only knew that in a town that had few Mormon kids Cam had found a group of friends who weren't rowdy, and who always got home on time. She was grateful for that. Cam was sure his mom wouldn't understand the situation with his friends and why, because of the gang's fundamental intolerance—and really, when Cam was honest with himself, their fundamental meanness—he had to choose between the gang and Novi.

So he didn't even try to explain. He just knew things were going to be different from then on. He watched Novi from his place at the sacrament table during the entire meeting. Neither of them realized the great expectations Cam was putting on Novi; Novi didn't know the hero Cam was making of her, and Cam didn't know just how much his life was going to change.

As for Novi, she was fascinated with sacrament meeting. The Clarke parents had told her a little about it, but even though she was forewarned it was a completely new experience for her. Normal, everyday people got up and prayed and gave the sermons, or the talks, as Larry Clarke called them. Teenage boys blessed and passed the sacrament, which was obviously a serious ritual. There was nothing élitist about anything, as far as she could see. Novi got the impression that anyone could pray or speak – you didn't have to be rich or popular or well educated. She liked this.

And the music. The congregation sang "I Stand All Amazed" at the end of the meeting, and it sent shivers up and down Novi's spine. It wasn't perfect; she could hear a few loud, out-of-tune voices; but overall, what with people singing their different parts in harmony, it was hard for Novi to believe that these people just casually opened their hymn books and started singing. No rehearsals, no practicing, just automatic harmony. There was no room for cliques, or gossip, or judgment – all the things that, as far as Novi could tell, somehow crept in whenever people got together – but just singing.

After the meeting was over, the friends of the Clarkes made an effort to introduce themselves to Novi, even though they tended to stare at her hair. Of course, there were some near-angry, disapproving looks, but Novi realized that this was just part of the territory. Overall, people were very friendly and not the narrow-minded, stuffy people Novi expected churchgoers to be. As a small child Novi had gone to church with her mom, but the memory was faint, and since then her mother had often spoken harshly of the Mormons, calling them snobs. But Novi didn't notice that characteristic in this congregation. *I guess you can't trust a stereotype,* she thought.

Cam hurried over to where the Clarkes were sitting. "Hello, ladies," he said to Joanne and Novi. "You look simply ravishing today. May I be so honoured as to escort you to Sunday School?" Joanne and Novi both laughed, Joanne forgetting her troubles for a moment. They slipped their arms into Cam's and walked with great dignity and majesty to their classroom.

That night, Novi wrote in her journal before going to bed.

sunday january 5

all right, i have to admit, church was interesting. i mean, people going up to the pulpit and speaking, in front of everybody, as if it's no big deal. you wouldn't get me up there. the thing i couldn't believe was the music. of course, this isn't to say i'm going to join or anything. i do give those mormons some credit though, because i did my best to shock them and most of them were very casual about it.

and an interesting development. after what they call "Young Women's" (people say i'm strange!), cam, from the skating party, came up to me. he asked me — wait, i'll just write down the conversation as i remember it.

cam: are you nervous about school tomorrow?

me: yes! actually, it shouldn't be too bad. a few days of adjustment and i'm sure i'll be the most popular girl in the school. (cam laughs) hey, what's funny about that? (i laugh)

cam: if you'd like, i can kind of show you around, you know help you get settled. unless you want joanne to do that.

me: oh no. i'd love it. it'll save joanne the trouble. just between you and me, i don't think i'm too good for joanne's image. you're much braver than she is. i worry about that girl.

well, when i say this, cam gets all angry and protective. who knows why. he hardly knows me. i calmed him down and we talked for a while. he said he'd been thinking about me, about being different and everything, and he claims he wants to, well, i guess follow my example. i'm flattered, but i think maybe he's trying too hard.

oh yeah. we also talked about this thing called seminary. cam says that all the mormon kids go to this thing every week day morning and get this, it starts at 6:30 a.m.! i can't believe it. i admire their dedication but i question their sanity. sleep is pretty sacred to me.

so far neither aunt trish nor uncle larry has mentioned anything to me about going. if they do, i'm running away.

_____ Six

Novi was sitting at the kitchen table eating raisin bran when the back door slammed open and Joanne stumbled in.

"Joanne," Novi said, surprised. "Christmas holidays are supposed to rest you, freshen you up, rejuvenate you. You look awful."

Joanne scowled at Novi. "Thank you very much." She was hurriedly making herself some breakfast.

"Where on earth were you?" Novi asked.

"Seminary," Joanne said, her mouth full of cereal.

"Oh, yeah. Seminary. Six-thirty a.m., right? You're a better girl than I, Joanne."

"Yeah, yeah," Joanne grumped. Although seminary contributed to the bags under her eyes, the truth was that she hadn't slept well the night before. For the longest time she'd been unable to get to sleep, while thoughts of the disasters the new day would bring swirled in her brain. When she finally slept, she dreamed that all her friends, her family—the world, in fact—had forgotten her. She went to school and her locker was empty. No one knew her or paid any attention to her. She went home and found that her room had been changed around and her family didn't know who she was. She went to church, and everyone in the chapel turned to look at her as if to say, "Who are you? Why are you here?" The only person who knew her was Novi, and she said, "You wanted me to stay out of your life, so I'll stay out of your life." So there was Joanne: unknown, unnoticed, and completely alone.

It was a horrible dream; the kind of dream that often plagued Joanne, though usually it came in less intense forms. This dream, and the others like it, played out Joanne's worst fears, for she felt that without the gang she worked so hard to be a part of she would be left to herself, and as far as she was concerned, that wasn't much. *Why did Novi have to come?* she thought for the thousandth time. *Things were fine until she came along.*

After breakfast the family gathered in the living room for family prayer. Novi still wasn't used to this strange ritual. In fact, she had never really prayed before.

". . . And please bless Novi on her first day at school. Bless her with courage and a sense of calm as she meets this new challenge. . . ."

Novi felt a strange flutter as Larry said these words. She had never prayed for herself, let alone heard someone else pray for her. The nervous churning in her stomach eased a little.

Joanne hesitated before walking into the school. *This could be it,* she thought. *The end of my life.*

"Relax, Joanne." Novi had been watching her cousin. *I'm the one who should be nervous,* she thought. *She could at least be a little more tactful about showing the pain I'm supposedly causing her. If she wasn't so insecure . . . If she wasn't so spineless . . .* Novi stopped herself. There was no point in wasting her energy on Joanne's hangups, she decided.

"You don't get it, Novi," Joanne snapped, not even trying to hide her resentment.

"Come on. It's not that bad. Just show me to the office and I'm out of your hair."

34

This made Joanne feel guilty again. *Here's Novi on her first day at a new school,* she thought, *and I'm feeling sorry for myself.* Joanne smiled weakly at Novi and they went inside.

Cam was waiting for them. "All right, Joanne, if you don't mind I'd like to teach your cousin the ropes. I'll take care of everything."

Joanne brightened. Maybe she didn't have to feel bad after all. Novi was in good hands. She wished Novi good luck and went on her way.

But by the time she reached the next hallway Joanne's feeling of relief had subsided and guilt had set in again. *No matter how you look at it,* she thought, *I'm still abandoning her, whether Cam is with her or not. I'm such a jerk.* Joanne trudged miserably toward her locker. As far as she could see, there was no way to win. *If I stick with Novi I lose all my friends. If I stick with my friends, I feel terrible. What am I going to do?* she asked herself in desperation. The two choices—the two Joannes she could be, the two lives she could lead—ripped her apart at the same time as they closed in on her claustrophobically.

Her heart beat faster and her head began to pound as she walked through the halls of the school. When she turned the final corner of her journey she saw Buffy and Jill waiting at her locker. Their presence deepened her despair, but for the moment it also gave her the lukewarm comfort that her gang hadn't yet abandoned her, in spite of her unavoidable relationship to Novi. Joanne swallowed back the slight panic she felt and waved to her girlfriends, walking quickly down the hall toward them.

"Where's your cousin?" Buffy asked when Joanne arrived at her locker.

"Good morning to you too, Buffy. Hi Jill." Jill nodded. Joanne took off her coat and hung it at the back of her locker.

"Well?" Buffy pressed.

"She's with Cam. She understands the situation."

"Good. I thought she seemed like a reasonable girl. Too bad about Cam, though."

"What do you mean?"

"Well, it looks like he's a turncoat. I like your loyalty, Jo."

Joanne glanced at Jill and they exchanged looks of disgust. They were both sure that Buffy had picked up her style of speech from the afternoon soap operas; that somewhere some cliché-ridden scriptwriter was writing Buffy's lines for her. Joanne got her books from her locker and the three girls walked to class together.

"And to your left is the men's washroom," Cam said. "I'm afraid that's off limits." Novi laughed as they continued down the hallway.

"And to your right we have the general office. After you, my dear."

"Hey, let's have some respect," Novi joked. "You hardly know me."

"Terribly sorry," Cam said. "After you, my darling."

"Much better."

Everyone in the office—two secretaries and a bunch of teachers—looked up as Cam and Novi entered. It was a fairly conservative town, and people like Novi were a rare sight. Today Novi was wearing an incredibly baggy pair of orange pants and a Mickey Mouse T-shirt, with a big black cardigan over top. Her coat was three-quarter-length fake fur. And, of course, there were the ubiquitous boots and white hair.

"Can I help you?" asked a staring secretary.

"My name is Novi Kosnowski."

"Oh, yes. We've been expecting you." The secretary smiled and led them to the vice-principal's office, where she opened the door and whispered something to the person inside.

"Wait here," the secretary said, and she smiled again and walked back to her desk.

Novi and Cam were left standing there. Despite Cam's

presence, Novi was feeling very nervous. It was like the first day of grade one again, only without her mother's hand to hold. Novi looked at Cam and laughed to herself. He didn't even look like her mother. All her professions of confidence and independence seemed meaningless now.

Just then a smiling woman, dressed neatly in a navy blazer and skirt, came out of the office.

"You must be Novi," she said, offering her hand. "My name is Madeline Fletcher. Hi Cam. Are you designated guide today?" Cam smiled sheepishly, and the three of them went into the office.

"Sit down. Please."

There was silence while Mrs. Fletcher glanced at a file folder on the desk in front of her. Novi looked around nervously, first at a beautiful brooch on Mrs. Fletcher's lapel, a circle of silver with a single, sapphire-colored stone set in the center. Then she looked at two pictures in the corner: one, a movie still of Buster Keaton, the other, a photograph of five people with Groucho Marx noses on. The middle person held a pig with a big blue ribbon tied around its neck. Novi couldn't help smiling.

"That's my family," Mrs. Fletcher said. Novi looked at her. Unlike the rest of the world, this woman didn't seem to notice Novi's appearance. Novi smiled again.

"Well, Novi, welcome to our school."

"Thanks." Having discovered what seemed to be a kindred spirit in the unusual guise of a school vice-principal, Novi was feeling much better about things.

"I received a letter from the counselor at your old school, Novi. He assured me that you wouldn't have any trouble adjusting to any differences in curriculum that may exist. And I can see by your transcript that your marks are very good. So I don't think there will be a problem there, do you?" Novi shook her head.

"I don't think I have to warn you about the social climate of a small-town high school. I expect you realize that you might encounter some problems because of the way you look.

Things should be fairly harmless, but if it goes beyond that don't hesitate to come to me. I won't think you're a fink if you do. Okay?''

Novi glanced at Cam, then nodded.

''Obviously you've made friends already.'' Cam smiled sheepishly again and Mrs. Fletcher laughed. ''As far as I'm concerned, people can always use a good lesson in tolerance. You'll be good for them.''

Mrs. Fletcher gave Novi a list of her classes and teachers and instructed Cam to show her around. She wished them both good luck as she walked with them to the outer office.

''That's one groovy woman,'' Novi said as she and Cam walked to her first class. Knowing she had an ally in high places made life a lot easier.

Novi made it through the morning alive. There were the customary stares, the obligatory calls of ''Hey, weirdo!'' and ''Hey, punk!'' but Novi knew that in a few days people would get used to the sight of her. There were always a few who took a strange personal offense to her appearance, and they would doggedly tease and sometimes even threaten her, but she figured that it wasn't a very rough town and even the staunchly intolerant would eventually grow tired of the effort it took to effectively persecute her.

After her last morning class Novi went to the cafeteria, where she was meeting Cam for lunch. While looking for an empty table to sit at, Novi saw Joanne. And Joanne saw Novi. Joanne stood up, and for an instant Novi thought she would come toward her. But a confused expression took over Joanne's face, and she just stood there, transfixed. Novi looked away and walked to an empty table at the opposite end of the cafeteria from where Joanne and her gang were sitting. She sat with her back to them and did not turn around.

She was still sitting there, picking at her lunch and waiting for Cam, when two people approached her: a young man, his hair barely poking out of his head — like new grass from the dirt — wearing a tie-dyed T-shirt with a peace sign on the front, black jeans with big rips in the knees, and clunky black combat boots; a young woman, long black hair framing her pretty face in a wild and confused mass, the same peace sign T-shirt as the young man, with a faded jean jacket over top, ripped Levi's, and desert boots.

"Greetings," they said in unison. "We are a delegation from the planet Zorton. We believe you are a long-lost inhabitant of the now-destroyed city of Erggle. We believe you are our sister. Welcome to the strange and foreign place we must now call home." The two Zortonians then took turns in placing their hands on Novi's shoulders and lightly bumping their foreheads against hers.

Once over the initial shock, Novi started to laugh. "Who are you?"

"Can we sit?"

Novi nodded. She could tell she was going to be friends with these strange creatures. Life was definitely brightening.

The young man spoke first. "I'm Horace."

"I'm Leona."

"I'm Novi. I guess we've already exchanged the customary greeting, right?"

"We just didn't want a fellow Zortonian sitting alone and friendless on her first day of school."

"Very kind of you," Novi laughed. "Actually, I'm meeting Cam Wilson here, so I won't be alone."

Horace and Leona looked at each other in disbelief.

"What?" Novi asked.

"You're meeting Cam Wilson?" Horace asked. "It's got to be some kind of trick. You don't know his crowd."

"No, I do know his crowd. I went skating with them last week."

"You're kidding," Leona said.

"No. I'm staying with my cousin, Joanne Clarke. That's how I met Cam."

"Joanne Clarke is your cousin?" Horace and Leona started to laugh.

"Yes, I can certainly see the resemblance," Leona said. This sent them into a further fit of laughter, and soon Novi joined in. When Cam arrived the three of them were still laughing uncontrollably, tears streaming down their faces.

"What's so funny?" he asked. Novi kept laughing, unable to speak. For her this was a much-needed release from the stress she had been feeling all morning. However, Horace and Leona quickly grew serious.

"Uh . . . Novi. I guess we'll go," Horace said, eyeing Cam with contempt.

"No, don't go," Novi said, slowly regaining her composure.

"Don't go because of me," Cam said. His past contact with Horace and Leona hadn't exactly been friendly. Horace and Leona stayed where they were, but they were silent. Cam tried to make conversation.

"How did it go, Novi?"

"Fine. No problems." Novi looked at the others. "Hey. What's going on?" She could easily imagine what Cam and the gang had done and the kind of resentment Horace and Leona were feeling. No one spoke. Finally Cam couldn't stand it anymore.

"Look, guys, I'm sorry. I'm sorry for what I did. I was stupid. I admit it."

"No argument here," Leona said.

"So why are you here now instead of with your little gang?" Horace asked.

"I'm really sorry," Cam insisted. "All the time I was with those guys, all the time we were bugging you, I knew it was wrong. I felt bad. I guess I was too much of a wimp to change anything. So, I don't want to be a wimp anymore, okay?"

They both remembered that day in September when Cam and Doug and Todd had waited outside the school for Horace. The girls were there – the audience, the cheering section – taunting and teasing while their three heroes beat up on Horace.

Leona remembered too. She had been forced to watch helplessly while listening to the smug insults that Buffy, Jill, and even Joanne had called out to her.

"What are you guys talking about?" Novi asked. "What did you do, Cam?"

Cam looked at Horace, then down at his hands. He cracked his knuckles nervously. He didn't want Novi to know what had gone on.

"We . . . uh . . . well . . ." Cam couldn't finish.

"Nothing," Horace said. "Nothing happened."

"Nothing!" Leona shouted. "You call what they did to you nothing?" But she stopped. Horace's face was stern.

"Forget it."

"I really am sorry, Horace."

"I believe you."

When Joanne saw Novi standing at the cafeteria door, her stomach suddenly tightened in fear – as it does when you narrowly escape a car accident, or discover you've lost your wallet. She had forgotten about lunch time. Of course, Novi would come in the cafeteria and expect to eat with her. Joanne stood up, but she couldn't go any further. *She'll have to make the first move,* Joanne thought. *I can't.*

But instead of coming toward her, Novi turned away and sat with her back to Joanne at a table in the corner. Joanne felt sick.

"What's up?" Doug asked her.

She sat down and started to eat the peanut butter sandwich from her lunch bag.

"Nothing," she said, trying to smile.

Seven

sunday january 19

another sunday at the clarke's. this church thing is
getting to be a habit. my apologies to you, little coil
notebook, for neglecting you for so long. i guess i've
been busy. i survived my first week of school–cam
took care of me so i didn't have to roam the halls alone.
oh, and the first day of school also brought me horace
and leona. definitely kindred spirits. we are all of an
artistic bent. horace wants to be a musician, and leona
wants to be an artist. i can see us in ten years–me
with a couple of novels under my belt, leona with
shows in all the major galleries of the world, horace
storming up the top ten charts. actually, i think horace
and leona should have been born twenty years earlier. i
can see them on peace marches and at folk festivals,
just hanging out. they're real hippies at heart. so, i
guess that's my little circle of friends. i feel really lucky
because i can easily imagine coming here, not meeting
any kindred spirits, wandering sad and lonely through
the halls of the school with no one to talk to, no one to
sing in the cafeteria with, no one to back comb my hair
with. that would be truly horrid. yes, i'm very lucky.

i mustn't forget cam. he's severed all diplomatic ties with the old gang. which is good, i think. however, i'm not sure if he really knows what he's doing. i mean, most of the time he's fine but sometimes i catch him looking at me, like he's waiting for my approval or something. i'm flattered, but what does my approval mean. oh well, i guess everyone does that. i guess i do that. it is nice to have someone to do things with. come to think of it, we do spend a lot of time together. studying, goofing off, going to church. sometimes we just talk. it's nice to have someone to just talk to.

anyway, enough of that. it seems horace, leona, cam, and i have become the prime targets of joanne's little gang. i think they're offended at cam's almost overnight abandonment. so they spend a lot of their time trying to get under our skin. nothing serious, just name calling, snide remarks yelled across the cafeteria, the occasional snowball, stuff like that. pretty harmless, but it's annoying. we tried to find a remote corner of the school to eat our lunches in but that didn't work, so we're back in the cafeteria. i figure if we ignore them, they'll get tired of us. right? besides, horace the ghandi follower doesn't believe in retaliation. so we wait until the gang gets tired of us.

which brings me to joanne. my crazy mixed up cousin. her friends make her join in on the teasing. i guess they can't make her, but she feels like she has no other choice. anyway, the poor girl has this look of misery on her face all the time. and she sends these little apologetic looks our way whenever she can. i can tell she's torn. i'd like to knock some sense into the girl. i don't know why she takes it.

why, i ask myself, haven't i heard from mom or dad? am i that easy to forget?

_____ Eight

"Oops! Sorry, Cameron, old buddy."

Cam gritted his teeth and walked to the table where Novi, Horace, and Leona had already started to eat. It was noon in the cafeteria—the main battleground for the war that was heating up between Joanne's friends and Novi's.

Actually, it wasn't a war. Horace believed in nonviolent resistance and he insisted that the most effective way to stop the attacks was to ignore them. The others reluctantly agreed. So the gang would dish it out, and the small band of rebels—Novi, Cam, Horace, and Leona—would take it.

"Come on, Cam, that's an old trick," Leona joked. Todd had tripped Cam, and Cam had barely avoided spilling his tray full of food. Cam scowled at Leona.

"Relax, Cam," Novi said.

"I'm glad you guys are so calm about it."

"What good is fighting back going to do?" Horace asked. "You know they'll win that way."

"Not necessarily. Two against two is a fair fight."

"But I'm not fighting."

Cam was getting angry. His honor and dignity were at stake. "Why is that, Horace? Are you weak, or just chicken?"

45

Horace looked down at his food. Nobody spoke. Cam regretted his words as soon as he had said them. "I'm sorry, Horace. I didn't mean that at all."

"There's no point in getting mad at me," Horace said quietly. "I didn't trip you."

"They've got to get tired of us eventually," Leona said. "I mean, how much fun can it be bugging us when we ignore them?"

Novi silently watched Cam. She was worried about him. He was new to this kind of thing, new to being on the receiving end of cruelty, and he hadn't developed patience, or thick skin, as she and Horace and Leona had. *One of these times,* she thought, *he's going to turn around and slug Todd or Doug and then he'll get it good.*

"Cam," she said. "You have a nice face."

"What on earth does that have to do with anything?"

"I mean, you have a nice face, so don't be stupid and let those gangster wanna-be's have their way with it."

"Yeah, Cam," Leona piped in.

"Yeah, Cam," Horace said in his best Leona voice.

Cam laughed grudgingly, but his anger remained. "I'm not going to take it much longer, you guys."

"But Cam," Horace said. "You have to."

"Why do I have to?"

"Because. You just do."

And Cam knew Horace was right.

That afternoon Cam and Novi were sitting at a table in the corner of the library. They had a free period together, and they always met here to study.

Cam was having a hard time in concentrating. Now that he was on the receiving end of the gang's systematic and continual persecution, his perspective was really changing. *How could I have been so stupid before?* he thought. *How could I have joined in on all those stupid stunts with the gang? Did I think I was cool, or something?* Cam thought of all the cruel things he had said, all the feelings he had hurt, the punches

46

he had thrown. *We'd sit there,* he thought, *and watch everyone walk by, give them the once-over, see how they measured up to our petty standards. Who did we think we were, anyway? And I'm supposed to be a Christian. How could I have blessed the sacrament when during the week I was a mean, judgmental jerk?* Cam covered his face with his hands.

"Cam, what is it?" Novi asked.

"I feel sick about what I used to do. I knew better, but I did it anyway. I just can't figure out why."

"Well, you don't do it now, do you?"

A muffled "No" came from behind Cam's hands.

"Isn't that enough?"

Cam dropped his hands and looked imploringly at Novi. "Is it? I hope so. I still feel sick just thinking about it. To tell you the truth, I don't know how Joanne can stand herself. I don't know how you can stand to live with her."

"I don't think she *can* stand herself. She's pretty miserable."

"Well, then, why doesn't she do something about it?"

"I don't know. I guess she's too afraid to change. She's not the most secure person I've ever met. I think she's afraid that if she stops joining in she'll get kicked out of the gang, which is probably true."

"So what? As far as I'm concerned, those guys aren't worth the effort."

"Well, what made you stay?"

"I didn't know the alternatives."

"Maybe she doesn't, either."

"But they're right in front of her. Anyway, I don't understand how you can stick up for her. She makes me mad."

"I understand how she feels. Of course, that doesn't mean I like her. We could be friends, but right now I have to admit I don't like her very much."

While Cam and Novi talked, the librarian, a short chunky man who bore a remarkable resemblance to Fred Flintstone, came out from behind a bookcase.

"Hey, you kids!" he said loudly. "This is a library. People are quiet here. People do not talk here. Understand? If you continue you will have to leave."

Novi and Cam contained their laughter just long enough for the librarian to disappear into the rows of books.

"Boy, you give a guy a little power and he goes nuts," Cam said as he laughed. It was several minutes before either of them could speak. They were sighing and giggling and wiping their eyes when they heard the librarian yelling at someone else in another corner of the library.

"Yabadabadoo," Novi said. And they were off again.

Novi did understand Joanne, and she watched while her cousin's unhappiness deepened, waiting for her to take steps to change her life. But as each day the situation stayed the same, gradually the pity Novi felt turned to impatience. But it wasn't only the unchanging situation. In addition, Novi resented the show she had to put on for Joanne's parents.

When she suggested the arrangement that night after the skating party, Novi had had no idea how complicated things would get. She had envisioned sharing a casual friendship with Joanne at home and then keeping a neutral distance while at school. But as it had turned out, Joanne's friends had destroyed any chance for neutrality, and Joanne herself had made even civility at home almost impossible.

Despite these difficulties, they had to make Joanne's parents think everything was fine. So they made conversation at the dinner table, talking about the last school basketball game, or the next dance, or their homework—boring, noncontroversial topics. They even spent the occasional evening in front of the TV together. And every morning they left the house together to walk to school.

But once they were out of Larry and Trish's sight, everything changed. At church they sat in their various classes without speaking. Their morning journey to school was silent, and they went their separate ways as soon as they entered the

48

school grounds. If their paths ever crossed during the school day they would pass by each other as if they were strangers.

"Joanne," Novi had said one morning as she and Joanne trudged through the snow to school. "We have to talk."

"Why?" Joanne muttered.

"Because our little agreement isn't working."

"It's working fine for me."

"Oh, yeah. I can see you're having a wonderful time."

As Novi said this, Joanne stopped walking. She looked down at her boots, then closed her eyes. She stood like that for a moment, her eyes squeezed tightly closed, her jaw clenched. Then she looked up at Novi, a strange mixture of despair and rage on her face. Tears were trying to force their way from her eyes.

"Novi," Joanne said in a low voice, rigid and barely controlled. "I'm fine, and everything is working out fine. Okay?"

Novi just nodded, and they started walking again. After this, Novi didn't interrupt the silence that Joanne held like a brick wall between them. *No use butting my head against it,* she thought.

"Novi, can I talk to you for a minute?"

Novi looked up from her chemistry homework and nodded to Trish. "Sure. What is it?"

"I'm worried about Joanne," Trish said. Joanne had gone straight up to her room after helping with the dishes, something she was doing more and more often of late. "I don't know what could be wrong with her, and I just wondered if . . . I don't know . . . if she's said anything to you."

"Uh, no, I don't really know of any problems," Novi lied.

"Well, does she talk to you about things like that? Is there something wrong at school?"

"Not that I know of. Maybe she's just tired from seminary."

49

Trish sat for a moment, staring at the floor. Novi watched her, hoping she would leave, feeling increasingly uncomfortable as her aunt's distracted silence persisted.

"Sorry I'm not much help," Novi finally said.

Trish broke from her stare and smiled at Novi. "Oh, that's okay. I'm just worried, that's all."

"Who is it?"

"It's Mom. Can I come in?"

"I guess so."

Joanne sat on her bed with her school books strewn in front of her. Her mother leaned against the wall and looked at her with concern. "Joanne, honey, is there something wrong?"

Joanne put on a smile. "No, Mom, I'm fine."

"Are you sure? You haven't seemed very happy lately."

"I guess I've been tired."

"Is that all? You spend so much time in your room, honey."

"Yeah, I've been studying a lot. I want to do well this semester."

"Are you sure there's nothing you want to talk about? You and Novi are getting along aren't you?"

"What does Novi have to do with anything?" Joanne stopped and cleared her throat to get the note of tension from her voice. She smiled again. "Really, Mom. I'm fine."

"All right. I just wanted to make sure. I worry about you, you know."

"Thanks." Joanne picked up a book, hoping her mother would leave. Her mother watched her for a moment, then left the room, closing the door behind her.

Joanne waited while her mother went down the hall, then down the stairs. It had taken all the control she could muster to keep calm as she talked to her mother. These days it seemed that she was always on the verge of crying. She tried to be cheerful, but it took so much effort that she could never

50

keep it up for very long. And as soon as her mother asked if something was wrong, all the tears she had been fighting back threatened to break loose in a torrent. All the sadness and loneliness she had been feeling seemed to gather inside her at that moment, and all she wanted was to let it out, to feel her mother's arms around her, to be a little girl again.

But she felt so far away from everyone that she was sure her mother's arms couldn't possibly reach her. And she couldn't let her mother know what was going on, so she had smiled instead. Now, as she listened to her mother moving about in the kitchen below, she was filled with a loneliness so intense that it was actual pain; the separation she felt from everyone she loved was so great and so dark that she thought she would be lost. Joanne could hold it in no longer. She shoved her books from the bed and flung herself down, burying her face in the pillow, and she cried as she had never cried before.

Now she's done it, Novi thought. *She's made me lie for her. It was bad enough acting it out, but now I've actually said it. Joanne, my darling cousin, you are definitely not worth lying for.*

Novi sat on the floor of the family room, exactly where she had been when her Aunt Trish left. With each second she grew more and more angry. *I'm a liar,* she thought. *I'm living a lie for stupid Joanne, who's too much of a wimp to take control of her life. She just lets other people run her life and drag her down, and now I'm letting her drag me down with her.* A glare fixed itself in Novi's eyes. She stood up, stomped up to Joanne's room, and pounded on the door. No one answered.

"I know you're in there, Joanne."

Still no answer. Novi flung open the door and opened her mouth, ready to shout the angry words she had prepared. But she stopped. Joanne was curled on her bed, her face hidden in her pillow, her body shaking with sobs.

51

Novi shut the door, went to the bed, and sat down beside Joanne. "Joanne, what is it?" she asked gently.

"Nothing," Joanne sobbed.

"You don't have to feel this way. You can change things."

"Please, Novi, go away," Joanne said, her face still buried in her pillow. "Please."

Novi sat where she was for a moment. She put her hand on Joanne's back, but she could feel Joanne stiffen, so she took it away. *I can help you,* she thought. *Just let me talk to you.* But Joanne didn't move, so Novi left her. She went to her own room and sat on her bed. She wasn't angry anymore.

_____ Nine

On Friday evening Joanne drove to Buffy's house. Her friends were already there when she arrived.

"We were just talking about Cam," Buffy said, after Joanne had greeted everyone and joined the circle of friends eating party food.

"Oh, yeah? What were you saying about him?"

"Oh, just that it's too bad about him," Doug said. "He was a good guy."

"What? Is he dead?" Jill asked, meaning to be funny.

"What do you think, Joanne?" Todd asked. "Is a guy who turns on his friends still a good guy?"

Joanne was starting to feel sick already. "Come on, you guys. This is old news. Besides, I don't think he's turned on us. I just think he has a crush on my cousin."

"No accounting for taste," Doug said.

Buffy laughed. "What some men won't give up for love, eh, Joanne? I had no idea that Cam was such a romantic."

Joanne laughed along with the others, but her heart wasn't in it. Eventually the conversation turned from Cam, much to her relief, and after everyone got tired of gossiping they played pool and then had a Ping Pong tournament.

Joanne was uncomfortable the entire time. In fact, she had wanted to leave as soon as she arrived. She only stayed because she was sure that as soon as she left they would talk about her, just as they had talked about Cam. So she tried to pretend that she was having a good time.

By eleven, however, Joanne couldn't stand it any longer. "Uh, Buffy, I hate to Ping Pong and run," she said, trying to make light of her exit, "but I'm getting a whopper of a headache. I think if I wait any longer I won't be able to drive." Joanne wasn't lying when she said this. The headache had started shortly after her arrival and had gradually worsened as the evening wore on.

"I can drive you home if you want," Doug offered.

Luckily for Joanne, she really did look sick, so her friends felt some pity for her. "No, I think I can make it. Thanks anyway." She said her good-byes and walked with Buffy to the front door.

"How about some advice?" Buffy asked Joanne just as she was about to leave. Joanne nodded weakly. "You'll feel a lot better if you relax, Joanne. We're your friends. Why are you so uptight around us? Unless, of course, you're thinking of following in Cam's footsteps." Buffy smiled sweetly at Joanne.

"Thanks, Buf," Joanne said. She quickly left, got in her car, and drove away.

Her parents were in the family room watching TV when Joanne got home. She didn't want to see them, so she just called to them from the bottom of the stairs. "I'm home," she yelled. "Goodnight."

"Hi hon," her father said. "Come in here."

Joanne rolled her eyes and went into the family room.

"How come you're home so early? It's only eleven-fifteen."

"I'm kind of tired."

"Are you sick, Jo?" Trish asked. "You look kind of washed out."

"I guess I've got a headache. I'm going to bed, okay?"

Her parents just nodded. She hated the concerned looks on their faces. It meant they wanted to pry into what was wrong, and she didn't want to let them in on anything. *It's none of their business what I do,* she thought. But as she was getting ready for bed Joanne had to admit to herself that the reason why she was guarding her privacy was that she was ashamed of what she was doing. She didn't want to talk to anyone. Not her parents; and she certainly didn't want to pray and talk to Heavenly Father. She especially wanted to hide her life from him.

So instead of kneeling down to pray, she went straight to bed. She just wanted to sleep. Except for her studies it was the only escape she had, and lately she had spent more and more time doing both.

Considering how anxious she was she fell asleep quickly, but it was a fitful sleep. She woke up when her parents came upstairs to bed, when Novi, who had spent the evening with Cam, came home, and when Scott passed her room to go to the bathroom. And Joanne dreamed such strange and disturbing dreams that night.

In one dream she was in a place she had only seen in photographs; a vast tundra field, with brown grass and treeless. She just stood there, lost, not moving, surrounded by empty horizon. It began to snow—huge, thick flakes soundlessly falling, quickly turning the brown field white, getting deeper and deeper by the second. Joanne woke up when the snow was at her waist.

She fell asleep again and dreamed that she was walking down a road in a desert. It was so hot that the road undulated ahead of her and the air shivered and rippled off the asphalt. Cars appeared in the distance and came toward her slowly. Finally they were close enough for her to see the faces of the drivers. Scott drove past her first; then Novi; then her father; and finally her mother. She had been waving and frantically jumping up and down, motioning for them to stop. She had tried to shout, but she had no voice. It was as if they hadn't even seen her. All she could do was watch the cars move further and further away from her and finally disappear with a shimmer over the horizon.

_____ *Ten*

saturday february 8

i don't want to complain, but I HATE MY LIFE. oh,
i know. i have friends. i have my health. but please.
first of all, there's the situation at school. yesterday
doug "accidentally" knocked my binder out of my
hands, resulting in a hallway full of my biology notes.
ha ha. very funny. and of course i had to convince cam
not to punch doug. i find myself forced into this kind of
diplomatic duty quite regularly.

then there's joanne. i'm supposed to pretend we're
best buds so that aunt trish doesn't find out that her
daughter is too spineless to do the right thing and admit
how petty and childish her friends are. but, on the
other hand, i feel bad for the girl because she's so miserable. the other day i went to her room, ready to yell
and scream, and i found her sobbing on her bed. i
mean, that room was practically throbbing with pain
vibes. so, i feel bad about being mad at joanne but i'm
losing my patience.

next complaint. i've been here for over a month and
neither of the aged parents has called or written. i

wrote mom a letter a while ago, but no word back. i'm beginning to wonder. i mean, are they ignoring me, or have i just slipped their minds? i can see it all now. the minute i got on the plane to come here, dad stepped out from the shadows and he and mom are now in bermuda celebrating how easy it was to get rid of me. well, maybe i'm being a bit paranoid.

anyway, suffice it to say that i feel rotten. i went to leona's tonight but i just couldn't get into things. i try so hard to be honest with myself and other people. i try to have integrity and do what i think is right but nothing seems to work out. horace would tell me to meditate or something. maybe i should try it. i joke about it all, but it's not that funny.

Cam was waiting in the hallway when Novi and Joanne came out of the Young Women class.

"Hi Cam," Joanne said meekly. Cam nodded.

"Well, I guess I'll see you later." Joanne tried to smile.

"Yeah, I guess you will."

Novi punched Cam in the arm. "Joanne, tell your mom I'll be home in time for dinner, okay?" Joanne nodded and walked away.

"Give her a break," Novi said when Joanne was out of sight.

"You give me a break. Why should I be nice to her?"

Novi looked heavenward. "Why should he be nice? he asks me. Here we are in a church and he's asking me why he should be nice."

Cam had to laugh. "You're right. I'm sorry. You must be taking notes here or something."

"I'm a very attentive student."

"What do you say I walk you home?"

"I was planning on it."

Novi and Cam were silent as they walked towards the Clarkes' house. The only sound was the creaking of the snow beneath their boots. Novi looked distractedly ahead while Cam gave her quick, concerned glances.

"Hey, Novi, what's going on? What's wrong?" Cam asked after a few minutes.

Novi looked at Cam and smiled. "Nothing."

"But you haven't said anything for five minutes. That's a bad sign."

"I don't talk that much," Novi said, and pushed Cam off the sidewalk into a snowbank.

"Hey, I'm wearing my good suit, you know."

Novi dug her heel into the packed sidewalk snow while Cam brushed himself off.

"I don't mind winter," she said after they started walking again, "except that I always slip on the snow. None of my shoes have any grips."

"I think you're avoiding my question."

Novi walked faster. "Turn here," she said.

"Where are we going?" Novi had turned off the road that led to the Clarkes' house and on to an unpaved side street that eventually led to a park. "Where are we going?" Cam asked again.

"This is the scenic route."

"Isn't it a little cold for that?"

Novi made a face at Cam and continued walking "It's just my family," she said, finally answering Cam's question.

"What about them?" Cam walked with his hands in his coat pockets, watching Novi intently.

"Well, my parents, they're . . . I don't know. Something's wrong with them. First my dad runs off, and now my mom is ignoring me. It just makes me feel rotten, I guess. I try not to let it get to me, but . . ." Novi didn't continue. By this time she and Cam had reached the park and were passing along a tree-lined ravine. "And I guess things are getting to me at school. I shouldn't let that bother me either. I guess my defenses are low."

"Yeah, I know what you mean."

59

Novi smiled. "Well, it's not that bad. At school, I mean."

"No. We can handle it. I don't know about your parents, though. Why don't you call your mom and try to talk to her about it. Maybe that would help."

"Good idea." Novi was silent for a moment. "Well, that's enough complaining for today."

"Do you feel any better?"

Novi picked up a handful of snow and threw it at Cam.

"I guess that's a yes," he laughed. "You're so violent, Novi."

Soon Novi and Cam came to a small field at the opening of the ravine. They walked to the bench at the top of the hill and Novi sat down.

"What are we doing here?" Cam asked. He remained standing, stamping his feet to keep warm.

"Uh . . . Cam," Novi said hesitantly, "I think you should know that I had a life before I came here."

"Does this have anything to do with what we were just talking about?"

Novi shook her head.

Cam looked at the ground. *Oh, great,* he thought. *She's trying to let me down easy.* "Well, what are you trying to say?"

Novi reached into her coat pocket and pulled out a pack of cigarettes, waving them in front of her.

Cam was surprised, even a little annoyed, but he laughed with relief. "I thought you were going to tell me you've got a boyfriend back home, or something."

"Would that bother you?" Novi teased as she lit a cigarette.

Cam turned away. He kicked at a mound of snow. "I don't know. Maybe. *Do* you?"

"No," Novi laughed. "Lighten up, will ya? We're starting to sound like a romance novel." She kicked some snow at Cam's leg.

"How come I didn't know you smoked?" Cam asked,

turning back to Novi and looking at her cigarette with barely masked distaste.

"Because I've tried to hide it from your delicate eyes."

"Why do you smoke, then, if you have to hide it?"

"Very good point," Novi admitted. "I never used to feel that way, though. I guess I had a few not very good reasons for smoking that seem pretty juvenile now. And I really am trying to quit. But lately I've been kind of uptight and I've run out of fingernails to chew, so here I am, puffing away."

"Just as long as you're trying to quit," Cam said firmly.

"I promise." Novi raised her right hand and lowered her head meekly.

"Cause I don't want to hang out with a girl with smoke breath."

"Okay, okay," Novi said, and she threw down the cigarette and ground it out with the toe of her boot. "Enough pressure already. Boy oh boy. You Mormons." But Novi was smiling. "Do you forgive me? Will you help me quit?"

Cam nodded. "You bet, honey," he said solemnly, putting his hands on Novi's shoulders as they faced each other. "And together we can lick this thing."

Novi rolled her eyes at him and stood up. "Enough, you geek! Let's go. I don't know why you dragged me out here. It's freezing."

"Very funny." Cam glanced sidelong at Novi and cleared his throat. "If the mademoiselle is cold, then perhaps I could keep her hand warm for her?" he asked. Novi looked at him and smiled. She slipped her hand into his and they started for home.

That night after dinner Novi went into the living room, where her uncle and aunt were talking together.

"Uh . . . Larry," Novi said timidly. "Do you think I could phone my mom?" She added quickly, "Collect, of course."

"Oh, sure," Larry said, smiling. "That's a good idea."

"Tell her hello from us," his wife said.

Novi went into the kitchen. She looked at the phone for a minute, preparing herself. She felt silly at being nervous about phoning her own mother, but she honestly didn't know what to expect. The last time she had seen her mother, when she dropped Novi at the airport, things hadn't gone very well because, as Novi figured it, her mom was too upset to think about how she was treating Novi. *This is silly,* Novi said to herself, and she picked up the receiver and dialed the number collect. Her mother answered, accepted the charges, and the operator got off the line.

"Hi Mom," Novi said excitedly.

"Novi?"

"Who else, Mom. You only have one kid, remember?"

"Well, hi."

"Hi. It's good to hear your voice, Mom. I miss you, if you can believe it."

"Well, I miss you too."

Neither of them spoke for several seconds. Novi nervously pulled at the phone cord.

"Did you phone for anything in particular, Novi? Do you need something?"

"Oh, no, I'm fine. I just wanted to find out how you are. How are you? Are you okay?"

"Yes. I suppose."

There was another silence.

"Uh, Novi, I can't really afford this call, dear. Why don't you write me a letter, or something."

"I did."

"Oh. Oh, yes. Well, this is costing money, so you'd better go. Say thanks to Trish and Larry for me."

"Yeah."

"Okay; bye, honey." Her mother hung up.

Novi stood for a minute holding the receiver, the dial tone blaring in her ear. Then she hung it up and ran upstairs to her room.

"What is wrong with my sister?" Trish asked. "What could she be thinking?" She and Larry had been able to hear Novi's phone call, and it was all too obvious that it hadn't gone very well. "Apparently she isn't thinking of Novi."

"Poor Novi," Larry said.

"Larry, why don't you go talk to her."

Larry nodded and went upstairs. "Novi," he called gently, just outside her room. "Can I come in?"

"I guess."

Novi was sitting on the edge of her bed with her back to the door. She was crying.

"I guess that call didn't go too well, eh?" Larry asked gently.

Novi shook her head.

"May I sit down?"

"I guess," she sobbed. He sat on the opposite side of the bed and talked to Novi's back.

"I don't know exactly what was said, but it sounded like your mom might have been a little insensitive."

"A little," Novi huffed.

"Do you think your mom is happy?" he asked.

Novi shook her head and sniffed. He handed her a tissue.

"I know that when I'm unhappy I don't always think about how others are feeling, or about how I may be affecting them. If your mother was happier I'm sure she would have been more sensitive, but she's having an awfully rough time right now."

"Well, it's not exactly fun for me," Novi said through her tears.

"I know. But I've been watching you, and you're very strong. You're also very thoughtful. You've been kind to Joanne, even though you have enough problems of your own."

Novi had to laugh at the irony of this. *If he only knew,* she thought.

"You know what helps me, Novi?" Larry said. "When I've got problems, I pray."

"Oh, sure! That'll help me a lot."

"Can it hurt to try?"

"I don't even know how to pray."

"You've had family prayer with us every morning. Just tell Heavenly Father how you're feeling. Ask him to help you cope with this. Ask him to help your mom too."

"She's supposed to be helping me. She's the mother. She should be comforting me, or something, not shipping me off to relatives. Why should I pray for her?"

"Because she's your mother and you love her. I think she needs all the help she can get. She's pretty unhappy. She loves your dad and she misses him so much that I don't think she can think about anything else right now."

"Does she think I don't love him?" Novi cried. "Does she think I don't miss him? He left me too, and . . ." Novi began to cry in earnest again and couldn't finish the sentence.

Larry looked at his niece, her body shaking with sobs. "Novi," he said as he moved beside her and put his arm around her. "I'm so sorry. I'm so sorry, honey. Trish and I love you, you know. We love having you in our home because you're so cheerful and kind and you make life interesting. We never know what you'll come up with next. I'm so sorry these things are happening to you."

They sat together for a while, until slowly Novi's crying subsided.

"Novi," her uncle said. "Your Heavenly Father loves you, too. Pray to him and he'll help you and your family, or at least he'll help you deal with the not-so-great decisions other people are making right now. Okay?"

Novi nodded and tried to smile. "Thanks," she said as he stood up to go.

"I'd ruffle your hair right now, only I'm afraid my hand would get stuck."

Novi laughed, and Larry left the room.

_____ *Eleven*

The next day Novi felt better. She didn't know whether the praying had anything to do with it, but for some reason she couldn't pinpoint she thought it did. She could honestly say to herself, and believe it, that whatever was going on with her parents, she was not to blame. She couldn't deny the fact that what her parents did affected her — whenever she thought about them a dull ache set in somewhere at the center of her heart — but she didn't have to feel guilty about anything. *This is their screwup,* she decided. *I have to get on with things.*

And that Monday morning as she turned a corner in the school and saw Cam waiting by her locker, she couldn't deny the tiny rush of excitement she felt. She walked a little faster.

"Good morning, luscious," Cam said. "Are you feeling better today?"

"Was I sick?" Novi asked as she dumped her books in her locker.

"You were kind of sad yesterday."

"Oh, yeah. Yes, I'm better today. In spite of your advice, I must say."

"What do you mean?"

"Well, I called my mother, like you said, and it was an absolute disaster. The woman sounded like she'd had a lobotomy. I said "Hi Mom," and she actually had the nerve to ask who it was. I'm an only child, for pete's sake. Anyway, after the call I had a good cry, and my good old surrogate father, Larry, talked to me for a while, so I'm okay. Actually, this morning I'm feeling quite fine."

"Good," Cam said. "I'm glad. Now that you're here I'm quite fine too." He took Novi's hand as they walked down the hallway toward class.

On Wednesday, during their free period, Novi and Cam were in the library studying. So far it had been a tease-free week for Novi and her friends. Except for the occasional dirty look, Buffy's gang seemed to have forgotten them; there was a sense of relief in the air, as if unwelcome guests had finally left after a painfully prolonged visit.

As for Cam, the few days of peace had allowed him time to think. When he was with Novi, Horace, and Leona, he felt plain and dull and talentless. The three others were creative and knew what they wanted to do with their lives, but he, although a good student, didn't stand out in any particularly interesting way, as far as he could see. When he first met Novi he had vowed to change things, but all that had changed were his friends. He was the same old Cam.

"I'm bored," he said, after watching Novi for a few minutes. This is how they usually spent their free periods. Novi would study, and Cam would watch her and interrupt her.

Novi looked up at Cam with mock annoyance. "We're sitting in a library doing math questions. Of course you're bored."

"No, I'm talking about the big picture," Cam explained. "I'm bored with my life."

"We're in high school in a small town. What do you expect?"

"Okay, okay. I guess what I mean is I'm bored with myself. I'm boring."

"Oh, well, there you go," Novi teased, reaching across the table and ruffling Cam's hair.

"Ha, ha," Cam said. "Thanks for your support."

"Well, what are you going to do about it?"

"I don't know. I thought maybe I'd get a haircut."

Novi flinched. "Ooh! Wait! Don't move so fast. Take it easy. I mean, the world will have to adjust."

"You know, Novi," Cam retaliated, "sarcasm is not very attractive in a girl your age. Remember that." Cam lightly kicked Novi under the table and she got him back with a pointy boot to his shin.

"Ouch!" He winced. "Those things could maim." Novi laughed and went back to studying, while Cam rubbed the pain from his leg. Looking at Novi, Cam again vowed to make some changes, then turned his attention back to the math problem he had been working on.

It was Novi who interrupted next. "Cam, do you pray?" she blurted out.

Cam looked up, surprised at Novi's question. "Pardon?"

"I was just wondering if you pray," Novi repeated.

"Yeah. Why do you want to know?"

"Just curious."

Cam waited for Novi to continue, as he could tell by her face that she wanted to. For some reason Cam hadn't previously thought about Novi asking about the Church. He just hadn't thought of her in terms of religion. Also, the fact that she came to church every week lulled him into forgetting that she wasn't a Mormon. All his life he had been taught to do missionary work, and his own full-time mission wasn't very far away. And yet for some reason he had never made that leap with Novi—that is, thinking of her as a potential investigator. *If I believe it's true,* Cam reasoned, *it has to be true for everyone. Why would I think Novi is exempt or that she doesn't need or deserve the truth?*

Cam looked at Novi. They had both been silent for a while, lost in their own thoughts. They smiled, embarrassed.

"What were you saying?" Cam asked, thinking he might have missed something.

"I was going to ask why you pray."

"Well, to talk to Heavenly Father, I guess. That's the sort of basic reason."

Novi nodded appreciatively. "I really like that. Other people say God. You Mormons say Heavenly Father. That's nice." Novi pondered this for a second. "But then again, I guess I'm kind of looking for father figures."

"Nothing wrong with that."

"Maybe not."

Novi paused again, thinking, and while she did Cam said a short, silent prayer asking for help to say the right things to Novi. Thinking of Novi as a Mormon made his heart burn.

"Does praying do any good?" Novi finally asked. "I mean, practically speaking."

"Since when have you been practical," Cam teased.

"Oh, shut up! I'm trying to be serious."

"I know. I'm sorry. Yes. I believe praying does good. I mean, it does accomplish something."

"What?"

"Well, we believe that when we pray there is someone actually listening and responding. When we pray we can get real answers, real blessings." Cam paused, trying to piece together what he actually knew about prayer. "But the thing is that praying depends on a lot of things. You know, like faith and stuff. And also, we don't always get the answers or blessings we want or ask for."

"Why?"

"I guess, because—well, what do we know, really? I mean, God knows everything, including what is best for us—a lot better than we know. We know what we think is best for us for, say, the next ten minutes. But God knows best in the long run. Also, everyone has their freedom, and I can pray until I'm blue in the face for something like . . . I don't know . . . like Doug not bugging me anymore, but if he still chooses to do it, then the only thing I can do is change the way I feel about what he's doing.''

Cam stopped and looked at Novi, who was listening so intently that her forehead was crinkled and she was biting at her lower lip. ''I'm going to have to think about all of this,'' she said. ''I've never really included God in my formula, you know, of how life works.''

Cam reached across the table and took Novi's hands in his. He didn't say anything; no words were required. He knew in an instinctive way that words would only shift the meaning of what was happening, diminish it, make light of it. Cam felt suddenly older than seventeen, and he felt closer to Novi than he had ever felt to anyone outside his family.

That night, while he showered and got ready to go to Leona's where the gang was meeting, Cam was doing some serious thinking. It was something he realized he hadn't ever really done before he met Novi. It wasn't as if he didn't have a lot of serious things to think about, but just that he had always floated along through life, taking on his parents' beliefs, doing what his friends did, living in a state of semi-consciousness. At least, that's how he saw it now.

Talking to Novi today, Cam had realized as never before that the gospel wasn't just something his parents believed in. He believed in it too. Today he had discovered his own testimony, previously lying dormant and untried under the mass of others' testimonies, and under all the Primary, Sunday School, priesthood, and seminary lessons he'd ever had; all of which it seemed he had sat through as if asleep. But he felt himself awakened now—awakened and facing not only his own beliefs but also his own ignorance. *What do I know about my own religion?* he wondered, ashamed. *Here I am trying to answer Novi's questions when I don't know anything myself.*

For Novi, Cam wanted to learn more, to think more, to see more clearly, to act more nobly—because another thing he had realized that day was that he loved Novi. He didn't even care if it sounded corny. To Cam, it didn't feel like just a crush or a whim or a high school fling. No one had ever made Cam think about everything as Novi had. No one had ever forced him to look so deeply into himself and the world around him. He felt as if Novi had opened his eyes, and not only that but also whole regions of himself that he had never known existed. He didn't tell her all he was feeling. He couldn't. But he wanted to, and that was something he had never experienced before.

And because of all these things Cam wanted to do everything, anything he could, to get closer to Novi. The whole physical thing was only part of it. When his parents had realized that he and Novi were seeing each other they had made him sit down with them and review the Church's doctrine on morality. Cam had rolled his eyes and reminded his parents about all the chastity lessons he'd ever had; but he had listened, and he knew his parents were right. He had somewhat shyly and in a roundabout, embarrassed way explained things to Novi, hinting at what he was feeling for her and what he couldn't, and wouldn't, do. She understood and jokingly vowed to make sure he stayed pure; joking, but serious as well.

But that was only part of getting closer to Novi. He could feel her inching slowly towards the gospel, and he wanted to meet her halfway and hurry her along. He wanted to identify himself with her in more ways than just holding her hand. He wanted to be more like her. And that was why he had suggested this evening's activities to the gang, and that was why he was going ahead with his plans. He could feel himself changing on the inside—his outlook, his very self—and he wanted the outside to match. Tonight he would be transformed.

Joanne was in her room, putting on her makeup. *It should be all right tonight,* she thought. *Just the gang. We'll eat party food, play a few party games, talk. We'll go to the dance. No hassles, no problems.*

Despite these efforts to reassure herself, however, Joanne was worried. After Cam's defection, things had really started to get out of hand. Doug and Todd were angry and spiteful, and Buffy — well, she was always trying to prove something. But then this week things had changed, and the tricks and teasing had stopped. Joanne didn't know what was going on, but she had felt their nervous excitement all week and she just knew they had plans for this evening. It was the school Valentine's Day dance and therefore the perfect setting for a showdown, since Buffy was so fond of that kind of obvious irony.

No one had mentioned anything to Joanne about their specific plans for this evening, and she had a terrible suspicion that whatever was going to happen was not only intended for Cam but for her too. She had been acting increasingly uncomfortable lately — she tried not to, but she couldn't help it — and she knew the gang could feel it. *Tonight they're going to test me,* she thought. *They've got something horrible planned and they're going to make me join in.*

Joanne sat down on the bed and looked around at her room. A dresser, a desk, a bed, a bed table, a reading lamp, a bookshelf. The only things on the walls were a full-length mirror and a picture of Christ. Suddenly Joanne realized that this was the most boring room she had ever seen in her life. And suddenly she knew that this most boring of rooms was a very accurate reflection of herself.

At the thought of what she considered her own utter dullness, at the thought of the impending disaster she knew this evening would be, at the thought of the total wretchedness of her life, Joanne started to cry. *How did I come to this?* she asked herself, knowing how melodramatic the question seemed. But she really wondered, *Have I always been this personality-less? What have I been doing with my life that at seventeen I still have no personality?* She thought of Novi, who was always cheerful and was obviously an individual, with her own tastes and opinions. *I don't even know what I think about things,* Joanne thought.

Just then, Novi knocked on her door. "Time to go, Jo," she said.

"Okay," Joanne said, trying to sound composed. She had tried to think of an excuse to tell her friends to get out of going tonight, but she couldn't. *This is supposed to be a fun social activity,* she thought. *Why am I going if I'm dreading it like this? What's wrong with me?* She had been asking this question a lot lately. Slowly it was becoming clear to her how ridiculous her life with the gang was, but she couldn't bear the thought of trying to change anything. *What's out there for me if I leave them?* she thought. *Nothing. Social outer darkness.*

So she stood up, took one last check in the mirror, and tried to shove from her mind the feeling that she was wearing someone else's clothes, thinking someone else's thoughts, holding someone else's opinions, none of which fit her and all of which made her feel like an impostor. She tried to put her face right so it didn't look as if she had been crying, and went downstairs.

Novi was waiting for her. She had a more slaphappy approach to dressing, so she was always ready first. She was looking particularly strange tonight. Her eyeliner extended to her hairline in a kind of spiderweb pattern, and her lips were redder than they had ever been. She wore a black miniskirt with opaque black tights-almost-pants underneath. And a big African print shirt—every color imaginable splashed on in every shape imaginable.

Joanne shook her head when she saw Novi. The contrast between Novi's wild and fascinating outfit and Joanne's preppy and, she thought (with a new view of her own sense of style), completely boring clothing was very painful to her. She tried to put it out of her mind. *I'm going to have fun tonight,* she decided. *Even if it kills me.*

"We're leaving!" Joanne yelled.

Larry and Trish came to the front hall to see them off. They laughed when they saw Novi. Her appearance was a constant source of entertainment for them. As long as her clothing was modest, they couldn't complain.

"My, but you're looking strange this evening, Novi," Larry said.

"Why, thanks, Unc." Novi grinned.

"What time does the dance end?" Trish asked.

"Midnight," Joanne said.

"What do you think, hon," Trish asked her husband, "should we give these girls an extra half hour?"

"Sure, what the heck." he answered.

"Wow. Great. Thanks," Novi gushed. "Did you hear that, Joanne? A half hour. A whole half hour. Wow. I can't believe it. Thanks. Thank you so much. Really."

Even Joanne was laughing when Novi finally stopped.

"Well, you kids have fun," Larry said.

"Okay, you adults," Novi said as she and Joanne put on their coats. They were about to leave when Scott came running downstairs.

"Wait!" he yelled. "I want to see you first."

Novi smiled and did her best fashion-show turn.

"Very weird," Scott said, delighted, at which Novi made a little bow. "How come you're so boring, Joanne?"

Joanne had to fight back tears as she and Novi left the house.

"So, what are you guys doing tonight?" Novi asked as they backed out of the driveway. Ever since seeing Joanne in tears, Novi had been trying extra hard to be friendly.

"Just a little party, then the dance," Joanne replied. Ever since Novi had seen her crying, and had tactfully avoided mentioning it, Joanne felt she had to at least converse with Novi. "What about you?"

"Oh, we have a few things planned," Novi said slyly.

"Oh." That ended conversation until they drove up to Cam's house, where the girls always went their separate ways.

73

"Well, have a good time," Novi said.

"You too." Novi got out of the car and Joanne drove away.

Novi, Cam, Horace, and Leona sat cross-legged on the floor of Leona's basement. Leona's parents, who, like their daughter, veered toward the rebellious side of life, had given Leona free rein of this section of the house, and Leona had created a perfect place where the four friends could meet.

The room was lit by four wooden cube lamps that Leona and Horace had made in shop in junior high. Round red and green windows let the light through, so it was a strange, colored light that came from the corners of the large room. Everything else was in shadows. Long strings of beads covered the doorways leading to the stairway and the laundry and storage rooms. Leona's own paintings (four splatter paintings, two chicken paintings, and an abstract portrait of Queen Elizabeth) covered the walls, and in some spaces Leona had dispensed with canvas altogether and painted the wall instead. The floor was covered with an ugly green shag rug that had once, in a tackier era, occupied the living room floor.

"Yes, I've made up my mind," Cam said. "I'm ready. I want you to do it."

Novi looked at him solemnly. "You've got to be absolutely sure."

"Yes, Cameron, my young friend," Horace said, trying to sound fatherly. "Once it is done, it is done."

"It's a big commitment," Leona added.

"Look, guys, I've given it a lot of thought. It's what I want."

The other three looked at each other, then nodded. "All right, Cam," they said in unison. "We'll begin."

Horace spread newspapers on the floor and put a chair on top of them. "Sit," he said to Cam.

"We will prepare for the ceremony," Leona said, and she and Novi went upstairs.

74

Horace had put on some music by the time they returned – something moody and Gothic. Then Horace and Leona and Novi gathered around Cam in the green-red light.

"Are you ready?" Horace asked.

Cam was silent for a moment, concentrating, preparing himself. "Yes," he said quietly.

"Who would you like to perform the ritual?" Leona asked.

"Novi, please."

So Novi took the scissors in her hand and cut Cam's hair.

When she had finished, they moved on to the next phase of Cam's transformation.

"We've prepared an outfit for you," Leona said. "It's yours to keep, as a gift on this momentous day. But from now on, you must make your own fashion decisions. Your clothes must be you, not us." Cam accepted a bundle of clothes from Leona and went into the laundry room to change.

When he returned, the others gasped with joy. "Turn around," Novi said. Cam paraded across the room in his new outfit and his new hair. The other three laughed and applauded.

"It's a success," Horace concluded. "Cam, my man, you're a real person now."

"You mean I wasn't before?"

"Nope."

Everyone laughed. Then Leona put up her hand to silence them. "Now," she said seriously, "it's time for the big test." She put her hands on Cam's shoulders and looked at him solemnly. "Cam, prepare yourself for the mirror."

"Yes, Cameron," Novi said, joining the game again. "Remember, we're talking major transformation here. Close your eyes."

They led Cam to a full-length mirror hanging on the far wall of the basement.

"Ready?" Horace asked.

Cam nodded.

"Okay, open thine eyes and behold."

Cam stared at the mirror in disbelief. His hair was short and bristly on the back and sides, and Novi had cut it spiky on top and back combed it for extra effect. He wore a paint-splattered T-shirt that Leona had designed for him, and a big-shouldered suit jacket from the 'fifties that her father had worn. He wore a pair of his old jeans that Novi had tapered and bleached to near-whiteness, and as a finishing touch Horace, Leona, and Novi had chipped in to buy him his own pair of desert boots, which he wore over a pair of thick, gray, work socks.

"I can't believe it," Cam said, in shock. "I can't believe it."

"Well," Novi asked, "what do you think?"

Cam just stared at himself in the mirror. After a few minutes the others started to worry. Maybe it was too much too soon, they thought. But then Cam started to smile, and suddenly he let out a loud whoop of joy.

"I'm free!" he yelled. And the four of them started to dance like idiots around the room.

"Come on," Leona said after a few minutes of celebration. "Come show my parents."

Mr. and Mrs. Findlay were in the kitchen playing Scrabble with Leona's younger brother and sister when the four teenagers burst in. Leona pushed Cam ahead of her. "Well, folks, what do you think?"

The Findlays looked at Cam with amused interest. Nothing surprised them anymore. "This isn't the same guy, is it?" Mr. Findlay joked.

"The very same," Cam said proudly.

"Well, I wouldn't have recognized you," Mrs. Findlay said.

"I don't know if it's an improvement," Mr. Findlay said, "but it certainly isn't boring."

"Exactly," Horace laughed.

"Okay, oldsters, we're off," Leona said to her parents as the gang of rebels bounced out of the kitchen. "We're going to introduce Cam to the world."

Mr. and Mrs. Findlay rolled their eyes as the four whooping kids left the house. "She's your daughter," Mrs. Findlay said.

"I wonder if Cam's parents know what he's up to?"

Driving to the school in Horace's car, Cam was so happy that he could hardly stand it. His new look invigorated him—he felt set free, as if he had been airlifted out of a deep rut that had prevented him from seeing how big and great the world was. The car was filled with upbeat music that made him bounce around in his seat. He itched for a dance floor, because there wasn't enough room in a car to be this joyful. Cam held Novi's hand and couldn't stop smiling. *This is what life's about,* he thought.

He rubbed his free hand over the newly short hair at the nape of his neck and looked out of his window as they drove through the streets of the town. It seemed so small to him—small and foolish, with no idea of the great world of ideas and change that he felt he was discovering. They sped past the familiar sights: the drugstore; the 7-Eleven on the corner; a row of houses; the gas station down the next street; more houses; a small, snow-covered park. Cam looked on, feeling above it all. Then he saw the chapel, a modest building with no steeples or crosses. A small corner of his heart protested against the joy he felt; a small wordless voice of warning spoke to him. He turned away from the window. The high school was just ahead.

_____ *Twelve*

The dance had already started when Joanne and her friends arrived at the school. They were feeling cocky and cool, sure of their place in the social scheme of things, and as soon as they had paid their three dollars admission they paraded onto the dance floor, with every move demanding to be noticed.

Except for Joanne. While the others spoke loudly and moved with exquisite smugness, Joanne tried as hard as she could not to be noticed. Her expression was practically apologetic, as if she was begging all onlookers to forgive her for associating with her friends.

In truth, Joanne was feeling embarrassed. Doug had arrived at their little pre-dance gathering with two six-packs of beer, and he and Todd and Buffy had drunk a couple each. Luckily for Joanne, Jill had declined all offers to drink, so she had company in her abstinence. Together they watched the three drinkers become more obnoxious with each sip. None of them held alcohol very well.

As if that wasn't bad enough, Doug had tried to insist that Joanne come to the dance with him in his car. It was always so hard for Joanne to stand up for herself if she ever disagreed with her friends, but she wasn't going to wimp out on this. So she and Jill ended up going together.

Not only was Joanne ashamed as she timidly danced in the big, hot, noisy school gym, but she was also worried. She had overheard the boys talking at Todd's house.

"But do you think they'll even show up?" Doug had asked Todd.

"Yeah, they'll show. Just keep your eye on them when they do, and if our buddy goes outside we'll meet him out there." The boys had laughed then, obviously thinking themselves clever and tough.

"You boys aren't planning anything mischievous, are you?" a smiling Buffy had asked as they were leaving for the dance.

"Who? Us?" Todd teased.

"Are you sure you're not coming with us?" Buffy asked Jill and Joanne. The two girls shook their heads. "Well, don't get lost on the way there," she laughed.

Joanne shivered as she thought about it. And she couldn't stop thinking about it as she danced, despite her efforts to forget everything and have fun. *Just look at them,* she thought, as she watched her gang dancing around her. *They're so transparent. They think they're being secretive and cool.* The boys kept looking at the entranceway, scanning the crowd, giving each other little conspiratorial glances. *Who do they think they're kidding?* Joanne thought. She would have laughed at them if she hadn't wanted to cry. Even though the dance floor was crowded and they were all pressed close together as they moved to the music, Joanne felt as if she was looking at them from a great distance. Finally seeing them in perspective, finally seeing how very small they really were. She wondered again how she had ended up here, with these people, and why she stayed.

"Hey, Joanne," Doug shouted over the music, "how come you're so low energy tonight? You should have had a beer with us." As for Doug, he had joined Todd and Buffy in a third beer just before they came into the school, and was feeling fine.

Joanne didn't say anything. She just smiled and tried to dance with a little more vigor. But when she caught sight of Novi standing alone at the gym door, Joanne abandoned her efforts at good cheer. She glanced at Doug and Todd, who had seen Novi also and were bouncing with excitement as they waited for the rest of Novi's gang to arrive. Joanne watched Novi, who stood for a moment looking out over the dance floor and then turned and faced the door.

Then Cam came in. Or rather, Cam was pulled in by Horace and Leona. He glanced timidly at the huge gym full of people and then was dragged onto the dance floor by Horace, Leona, and Novi.

Joanne was in shock. She had stopped dancing completely and just stood there trying to see Cam through the crowd, catching a glimpse of him every few seconds.

"Oh no," Jill said. She had moved beside Joanne, and they both stood there dumbfounded. "Oh no," Jill said again. Joanne turned to her, and they exchanged looks of terror. Doug and Todd were no longer bouncing with excitement. They were seething now, with genuine anger and disgust. Cam's betrayal was no longer just a joke. It was a slap in the face.

Buffy smiled archly. Cam's transformation didn't anger her; it pleased her. Now Doug and Todd would *really* get Cam. Now Joanne would *really* suffer. She moved beside Jill and Joanne.

"Hey, Joanne," Buffy shouted over the music. "What happened to your friend Cam?"

Joanne gulped. She still couldn't believe her eyes. "I don't understand," she said to no one in particular.

"Let's just dance," Jill said, trying to rescue Joanne from Buffy. "Come on, guys, let's just dance. Who cares about the weirdos." Jill tried to pull Todd and Doug into movement, but they refused to dance. They stood stock still, glaring across the crowd at Cam. Waiting for him to make the first move.

Novi, Cam, Horace, and Leona stood outside the gym, where they could hear that the dance was already in full swing.

"Come on, Cam," Leona urged. "I want to dance."

"People are going to stare at me," Cam said, his boldness slipping away at the thought of a gym full of people.

"So what?"

"I'm going in," Novi said, and she did. Leona and Horace waited for a minute, then they each grabbed one of Cam's arms and pulled. Finally, after a struggle, they went into the gym.

"Here we are," Horace said. Cam stood there shyly, waiting for everyone to start staring at him. Actually, hardly anyone noticed them. The three veteran rebels quickly lost patience and dragged Cam onto the dance floor.

"Just have a good time," Novi yelled. "Forget about everyone else."

"Feel the music," Leona said, her eyes closed, her body swaying crazily. "Feel the music. Let it fill your soul."

Cam laughed and loosened up a bit. "Who are you? Melba the Disco Queen?" At that they all started to do their best disco steps, and soon Cam forgot that he was uncomfortable.

They had been dancing for a while, oblivious to everyone else, wrapped up in their own zaniness, when Novi leaned over to Cam and asked if he would go outside with her.

"We're going for air," she shouted as they left Horace and Leona to themselves. Novi took Cam's hand as they walked down the hall toward the nearest exit. She sang along softly to the music that seeped out from the dance.

"What's up?" Cam asked.

"It gets so stuffy in there. All those frantic teenage bodies." Cam laughed. "Besides," Novi said smiling up at him. "I wanted an excuse to be alone with you, now that you look so groovy."

Cam thrilled inside. He had thought he was happy before, but things just seemed to get better. For the moment, the sense of foreboding he had felt in the car disappeared.

Todd and Doug were waiting outside when Novi and Cam left the school. Having seen Cam leave the gym, they had quickly used another exit and had run around the side of the school to intercept him.

"Oh, great," Cam muttered as soon as he saw Todd and Doug poised a few yards away from him. He realized that deep down he had been expecting this. "Judgment day has come."

"What are we going to do?" Novi said. In all her years of personal rebellion nothing like this had ever happened to her. She didn't know where Doug and Todd's endless supply of hatred came from.

"You go back inside and get Horace and Leona," Cam whispered.

"Why don't you just come with me? We can get back to the gym and find a teacher."

"Novi, they're not letting me back inside." Doug and Todd were slowly coming closer, taking their time, savoring the moment. I'll try to talk them out of . . ." Cam didn't finish. Novi gave his hand a little squeeze and ran to get the others.

Cam prepared himself for the confrontation. He turned for a second to look into the school, hoping someone might be there to help him. Instead he saw Joanne and Jill and Buffy peering out of the window at him. Joanne and Jill looked ready to cry. Buffy was smiling. Cam turned away from them and faced Doug and Todd, who now were right in front of him.

"Hi, guys," he said.

"Looking good, buddy," Todd said through clenched teeth. "Looking good."

Joanne, Jill, and Buffy were coming towards her when Novi came into the school. *I don't have time for these people,* she thought, and she ran right past them before they could stop her.

"Wait, have you paid?" the girl at the ticket table asked officiously. Novi flashed her hand, showing the place where the girl had stamped her earlier that evening, and then ran on.

"Don't run, please," the ticket girl said. Novi turned as she ran and glared at her.

Novi found Horace and Leona leaning against the wall, talking. They could tell by Novi's face that something was wrong.

"Oh, no," Leona said. "Where's Cam?"

"Todd and Doug, right?" Horace asked. Novi nodded, and the three of them ran from the gymnasium.

Thirteen

Joanne knocked on her parents' bedroom door.

"Come in, Jo," her dad called out.

Joanne poked her head in the room. "I'm home."

"Okay. Thanks for checking in. Did you have fun tonight?"

"I guess. Novi's staying at her friend's house tonight. She asked me to tell you."

"What friend?" her mother asked.

"Leona. Her dad teaches social and art. You know, Mr. Findlay."

"Oh, yes. Leona's a nice girl, isn't she?"

"I guess."

"Okay. Thanks, hon. Goodnight."

"Goodnight."

Joanne closed her parents' door. Somehow she managed to brush her teeth and wash her face and hang up her clothes, and somehow she ended up in her pajamas, kneeling beside her bed. But the thought of praying snapped her out of whatever trance she'd been in. Everything that had happened that night flooded back into her head and repeated itself in slow-motion, instant replay.

She watched again as Todd and Doug walked toward Cam and started to hit him. They took turns holding back his arms, and punched until he'd fallen to his knees. Todd had been holding his arms then, and he'd let them go, and Cam had fallen forward onto his hands.

Again, Joanne saw Cam on his hands and knees, his blood dripping onto the snowy sidewalk. Again, she saw Buffy smile and cheer the boys on. Again, Joanne felt a wave of sickness come over her. She had closed her eyes then, unable to watch anymore; and Buffy, seeing this, had said: "Come on, Joanne. Don't you like a good fight?"

When Joanne had opened her eyes again, Cam's friends were trying to rescue him from Todd and Doug, who were circling Cam, giving him a punch or a kick here and there, waiting for him to rejuvenate so they could start in on him again. The boys had turned to Horace and were begining to throw some punches at him too, when Joanne couldn't stand it anymore and she ran from the school begging them to stop. She was still yelling "Stop!" over and over, tears streaming down her face, when Todd and Doug finally did stop. Horace and Leona gently helped Cam through the parking lot to Horace's car.

Again, Joanne saw Novi's face as she came toward her, full of hurt and disbelief. It was the first time Joanne had seen Novi cry. "Tell your parents that I'm staying at Leona's." And then Novi walked away.

As she had turned to her friends Joanne felt a strange numbness, as though none of what she had just seen could possibly be real. The four stood together a few feet from her, watching. Jill alone seemed repentant. Buffy looked at Joanne, challenging her; and Todd and Doug, burning with hatred still, with defiant eyes dared Joanne to question what they had done.

Joanne had just stared at them. *What's wrong with you?* she wanted to yell. But instead she had turned away and walked toward the parking lot. When she looked back, her friends were gone.

She saw it all again as she knelt by her bed and two things became chillingly clear to her. As she thought of Novi's expression, Joanne realized how useless her one moment of protest had been. Worse than useless, her cries for Todd and Doug to stop, long after they'd already brought Cam to his knees, had been utterly selfish. She hadn't been able to stand it anymore; it had little to do with Cam. Joanne knew this, and so did Novi.

When Joanne thought of her friends as they stood together, facing her, she realized with a sickening feeling in her stomach that she didn't even know these people. She didn't know them and they didn't know her, and none of them cared one way or another. Joanne realized just how much time and self she had wasted with the people she had mistakenly believed were her friends. *Because in the end,* she thought, *here I am, alone.*

"Heavenly Father," she whispered, "I'm sorry. I'm so sorry."

_____ Fourteen

The next day, everything hit the fan.

It started out quietly enough: Scott left at eight-thirty for hockey practice; Joanne dragged herself out of bed early, finished her chores, then went directly back to her room; Novi came home from Leona's around ten-thirty, quickly did her chores, and then went directly to her room. It seemed to be just a placid winter Saturday.

But then, shortly after noon, the phone rang.

It was Mr. Wilson, Cam's dad. His wife was hysterical somewhere in the background, demanding Novi's head, Joanne's head, then Larry's and Trish's heads.

"Pete," Larry said, trying to understand what was going on at the other end of the line. "Pete, I can't hear you. What's going on?"

Hearing her husband's strained voice, Trish came into the kitchen and stood behind him, listening.

"Listen, Pete . . ."

"Yes, I understand, but . . ."

"Pete . . ." Larry was silent for a moment, listening. "Okay, Pete. Listen. We'll come over and sort this thing out, okay? We'll be right over." He hung up.

"What was that about?" Trish asked.

"I'm not sure," Larry replied, "but apparently there was some trouble at the dance last night."

"That's why it's so quiet around here. What happened?"

"I'm not sure. I gather Cam got beat up."

"That's terrible. But why are they calling us? Was Joanne involved? Or Novi?"

"I guess so."

"Well, how? Did they beat him up?"

Larry frowned. "Apparently things aren't quite as they seem. I think you and I are a little bit in the dark about the situation here."

"What situation?" Trish was completely confused.

"The situation that exists, which isn't at all like the situation we think exists."

"Oh!" They both shook their heads. "Sometimes I wonder if we know our kids at all," Trish said sadly. "I mean, there's so much they keep from us, so much we don't see. So many secrets."

Larry nodded, and hugged his wife tightly. They were silent for a moment, each trying to sift through the years to when they were teenagers with secrets of their own.

Larry broke the silence.

"Well, it's time for Joanne and Novi to come clean. Let's see what they have to say about last night."

The couple held hands as they walked upstairs to get the two girls. "It's a good thing," Trish said, grinning at her husband, "that we are so level-headed and reasonable. But I could do without these little adventures."

"But, honey, what would we do without a dash of teenage intrigue and violence every once in a while?"

"We'd survive."

Mrs. Wilson had managed to calm down. It was still hard to tell whether she was more upset about the damage Todd and Doug had done to Cam's face or the damage Novi had done to his hair.

"Look at my son!" she had shouted when the Clarke entourage arrived. Cam was slouched on the chesterfield in the living room and barely perked up even when he saw Novi.

"Hi Novi," he mumbled through swollen lips. Novi sat down beside him and gently touched his face. Cam looked awful.

"Oh, Cam," Trish said with concern. "Are you okay?"

"I'll live," Cam muttered.

"What's going on? What happened?" Trish asked.

"Ask your daughter," Cam growled.

"I'd like to know what your niece did to my son," Mrs. Wilson demanded.

"Me?" Novi protested.

"Yes. Look at his hair."

"Oh, that," Novi said, rolling her eyes.

"What does Joanne have to do with this?" Larry asked.

"She's the one who beat him up," Cam's mother said.

"What?" Larry shouted. Then everyone started shouting.

Finally Joanne spoke up. "Excuse me," she yelled, to be heard over everyone else. "Excuse me. Can I talk for a second?" Everyone in the room looked at her. "My friends beat Cam up. Novi's friends dressed him up. Okay?" With that, Joanne stopped talking and stared at the floor. She looked determined never to speak again.

"What do you mean, your friends and Novi's friends?" Trish asked.

Joanne said nothing.

"Joanne."

Still nothing.

Trish turned to Novi. "Novi, can you please tell me what's going on?"

Novi looked at the floor. The room was aching with tension. No one spoke. Joanne's parents searched the faces in the room for some kind of explanation. Pete Wilson's face was set in an apologetic frown. Mrs. Wilson looked at her son with a mixture of concern and exasperation.

Finally Cam couldn't stand it anymore. "Novi, why don't you tell your aunt about her daughter. Go ahead. I'm sick of this. She shouldn't be allowed to get away with this garbage any longer."

"Get away with what?" Trish asked Novi. "Go on, Novi. Talk to me, please."

Novi looked at her, then at Cam, then her eyes rested on Joanne, who was so still and expressionless that it looked as if someone had flicked a switch and shut her off. Novi continued to look at Joanne as she spoke. "Joanne . . ." Novi didn't like squealing on Joanne but, like Cam, she'd had enough. She went on. "Joanne's friends didn't want me hanging around because . . . I don't know, I'm weird, I guess. So they told Joanne she had to pick. Them or me. I told her to pick them."

Novi continued: "So we've been pretending we're friends to keep the peace at home. But really, Joanne's friends can't stand me and we can't really stand Joanne's little gang, either, to tell you the truth."

"Who's we?" Larry interrupted.

"Cam and I, and Horace and Leona."

"Go on, Novi," Mr. Wilson said.

"Well, that's basically the situation. Joanne and I pretend we're friends at home, then at school Joanne's gang spend their time trying to drive us crazy; and now, they've decided to beat us up too."

Novi was looking at Larry and Trish now. "But I'm sick of lying for your daughter. Her friends are jerks, and she's joined right in, so I guess that makes her a jerk too."

"Novi," Larry said firmly.

"I'm sorry," Novi shouted. "But it's true. I felt bad for her for a long time because she was unhappy, but how long am I supposed to just sit back and take it? She's been too much of a wimp to stand up to her friends. She goes along with all their little tricks, and last night she just stood there while they beat Cam up. I just can't pretend that I'm friends with her anymore. I'm glad you know, 'cause I couldn't have done it for another day. All this time I've tried so hard for her . . . you know . . . to let things go, and to try and not mind all the really mean things her friends do. Not once did she ever think about how I might feel." Novi leaned forward and buried her face in her hands.

Joanne was still absolutely quiet, but now tears rolled down her cheeks. She made no movement to wipe them away.

Eventually, everything got sorted out. Mrs. Wilson calmed down, and although still angry about her son's hair she realized he had decided he couldn't be like Todd and Doug; that he didn't want to be a bully, he didn't want to be cruel and mean. As the Wilsons came to understand the big picture, they realized that Cam had made a good decision in leaving that gang, and they were proud of him for that, at least.

As a result they grounded him for only two weeks instead of for a month. They decided that, after all, a month is a long time in the last semester of high school, and hair can always grow back.

Joanne and Novi received that same punishment. Joanne's sullen and silent behaviour made sense to her parents now. And they both knew that, although it didn't diminish the seriousness of what Joanne had done, she had already suffered a great deal because of her actions. They didn't want to make her suffer more.

As for Novi, she didn't think she deserved any punishment. "What did I do?" she demanded of Larry when he told her she was grounded.

"Well, you did cut Cam's hair."

"So? Cam can get his hair cut if he wants to. And I can do it. It's not against the law."

"Novi, I know it's been a hard time for you. Obviously it's been harder than we imagined. It was wrong of Joanne to put you in this position. I wish she could have made some different choices. But the point is, you lied to us too. This kind of deception is serious.''

"I know I lied. And it makes me furious that I did. But I just did it for your daughter. I knew it was wrong. I knew she knew it was wrong. That's why I didn't think it would ever go this far.''

"I understand," Larry said quietly. "Please try to understand my position. Why I'm doing this.''

Novi fumed in silence.

"Novi, can you forgive Joanne?" Larry asked as he got up to leave Novi's room.

Novi scowled at him. "Forget it. I'm just so sick of forgiving people. My mother, my father, Joanne. I'm sick of it. Why should I get all this garbage from everyone and then turn around and forgive them? Why can't anyone treat me the way I deserve to be treated? Forget it.''

Larry nodded and then left the room, closing Novi's door behind him, knowing there were some rules he could not enforce.

Fifteen

The next day was like a new bruise, tender and aching. No one spoke much to anyone else as the Clarkes got ready for church. Even Scott was sensitive enough to stay quiet, and the parents didn't attempt to make conversation as they drove to church. When they arrived, Joanne followed her family into the chapel and sat down without making the usual stops to talk to people. She just sat staring at nothing and feeling about as awful as she had ever felt in her life.

Novi told Larry and Trish that she would be sitting with Cam, and they judiciously decided not to object. She found Cam leaning against the wall by the water fountain.

"Hi you," Novi said. "How do you feel?"

Cam looked only minutely better than he had the day before, only the color of his bruises having changed much. "I don't want to be here."

"Why? What does church have to do with anything?"

"Nothing, I guess," Cam muttered. "But that's how I feel."

"Will you sit with me when you finish with the sacrament?" Novi asked as they walked slowly toward the chapel.

"I'm not doing it today," Cam said. "I'm not exactly in the mood for it, you know?"

Novi thought about this. She liked it when Cam blessed the sacrament. It somehow made him seem a lot older than seventeen. To her it seemed an important thing, even though she didn't fully understand it, and she didn't want Cam to just stop doing it.

Why do things happen this way? she wondered as she stood beside Cam in the hallway. *Cam's upset and angry, and he didn't do anything wrong, and Doug and Todd probably don't feel bad at all. Still, how long do I hang on to this? Look at what it's doing to Cam.* She didn't particularly like the taste left in her mouth by the bitterness she felt. Since talking to her uncle the night before, Novi's anger had begun to drain from her, as it seemed to take a concerted effort to hang on to it, whereas it was so much easier and felt so much better to just let it go. Seeing Cam just reinforced this; clearly he was acting closed and hard and seemed to be using all his energy to stay mad at the world.

On the other hand, seeing Cam, bruised and swollen, also reminded her just why she had been upset in the first place. Novi was torn between her sympathy for Cam's anger and her desire to just forget the whole thing. *But I guess it's easy for me to think about forgiving,* she thought. *I didn't get my face smashed.*

So in the end Novi decided it was too soon to stop being mad, and she looked at Cam's bruised and swollen face and tried to retain her grudge.

"You can sit with me the whole time, then," she said, grabbing Cam's hand again.

They were standing in the foyer, waiting till the last minute before going into the chapel, when Bishop MacInnes came out of his office.

"Oh-oh," Cam whispered, turning his back to the approaching bishop.

"Good morning, Cam," the bishop said.

Cam made a face before turning around. "Hi," he said sullenly.

"How are you doing?" the bishop asked.

"Been better."

"How are you, Novi?"

Novi just shrugged. She liked Bishop MacInnes, but she got the feeling that Cam didn't want to talk to him, so she kept quiet.

"Cam, could I talk to you after sacrament meeting today?" the bishop asked.

"Why?" Cam demanded.

"I just want to talk to you, Cam. Don't worry. I just want to talk." The bishop looked at Cam until he nodded reluctantly. "Novi? Do you want to come in and talk?"

"Uh, why?" she said nervously. The only reason she could think of for talking to the bishop was if she was in trouble. "What did I do?"

The bishop laughed. "You're not in trouble, Novi. If you want to come in, you can. If you don't want to, that's okay too."

"Maybe I'll take a raincheck, then," Novi said, relieved.

"Sure," the bishop said, smiling. "I'll talk to you after sacrament meeting, okay, Cam?" He touched them both lightly on the shoulder, then walked into the chapel.

"Great," Cam huffed as they followed the bishop, found a place on the back row of the chapel, and sat down.

Sacrament meeting was torturous. Joanne thought it would never end, and she was certain she couldn't make it through Sunday School, because she felt she was going to explode. She was just about to escape somewhere when Bishop MacInnes stopped her.

"Joanne, hi. Do you think you could come and see me in a few minutes?"

"What for?" Joanne said, suddenly feeling sick.

"Just to see how you're doing. In about twenty minutes, okay?" The bishop smiled and walked away.

Joanne was slightly grateful for a legitimate excuse to skip Sunday School, but more than anything the thought of a bishop's interview filled her with dread. She knew the only way she could get through it was to become a rock, mouth shut and feelings to herself. Which might prove difficult, because as it was she felt she would break apart if anyone even spoke to her. She repeated the word *control* in her mind over and over as she walked.

But then, as she left the chapel, she saw Novi and Cam in the foyer. Somehow she knew that they were waiting to talk to the bishop too, and that everything would come out, the terrible truth about her would be known. She stood staring at Cam and Novi for a second. Novi looked away, but Cam glared at her.

"I . . . I . . ." she stuttered, but as soon as she opened her mouth there was no way to stop the flood, and she burst into tears. Passing the bishop as he came out of his office she ran towards the coat rack, grabbed her coat, and ran out of the door.

"What happened?" the bishop asked Novi, after watching Joanne disappear.

"Should I follow her?" Novi was terrified.

"Forget it," Cam said. "She's flipped. She can't take the guilt."

"Cam," Novi said, hitting him on the arm.

"Hey, I don't need you getting on my case too!" Cam yelled.

Novi didn't say anything. She knew Cam was justified in his anger, but she couldn't stand to see Joanne so unhappy. She looked imploringly at the bishop, who responded by leading Cam into his office and shutting the door.

Walking home from church, Cam was silent. Novi wasn't sure what to say, but finally she spoke.

"What's going on in your head?"

"Nothing," Cam grumped.

"Come on, Cam. I like you better when you're a carefree, forgiving soul. Let it go, why don't you."

Cam stopped walking and faced Novi angrily. "Look," he shouted. "I'm really sick of everyone feeling sorry for Joanne, okay? *I* got beat up, not her. So if you want to make friends with Joanne, that's fine, but not while I'm around."

At this Novi got angry too. "I thought you were a Christian, Cam. Nice attitude."

"I thought Joanne was a Christian."

"Oh, that's great. Use Joanne as an excuse not to do what you know is right."

"I thought I was doing what's right, but then I get beat up and everyone's on my case to change my attitude. But . . . I mean . . . what about Todd and Doug? What happened to them? Nothing. It just doesn't make sense."

Novi could tell by his face in the seconds after he spoke that Cam was about to cry and was trying desperately not to.

"I've got to go. I've got to figure things out. I'll see you later." And he walked away.

Novi just stood there and watched him, his fists shoved in his coat pockets, his shoulders hunched and stiff. She knew how he felt. It wasn't fair. It didn't make sense.

But suddenly she also knew how Joanne had felt that day in January when Novi had arrived. How she felt at being forced into a choice between doing the right thing and friends in the wrong. And now Novi was faced with the same choice herself. She felt a dull ache beginning somewhere in her chest, because she knew that, until Cam could sort things out, doing the right thing might mean doing it alone.

Sixteen

thursday february 20

what a week i'm having. first there was the weekend from my worst nightmares – cam getting smashed up, joanne having a nervous breakdown, and all three of us getting grounded. i've never been grounded before in all my long career as a teenager. and now i'm caught between cam, who really does know he should let things go but still wants a justice he'll probably never get, and joanne, who needs someone pretty badly, i think. well, cam isn't ready to forgive, and doesn't want to go near joanne, or for me to go near her. not if i want to stay his friend anyway. what do i do?

my decision has been somewhat postponed i guess since joanne won't let me come near her anyway. i've seen glimpses of her at school, but she's always clutching her books to her chest, walking fast with her head bent forward, and only comes out for supper, which she barely eats then asks to be excused so she can go study. all i can say is she's going to do very well in school this semester. so am i for that matter. with cam in the state he's in, and being grounded, i've been getting a lot of studying done myself.

today i risked life and limb by going to joanne's locker to find her. luckily only jill was there. she smiled kind of apologetically at me, so i was safe. anyway, joanne's locker was empty, no lock on it. jill said she came to school on monday and the locker was empty then. but she didn't know where joanne had moved her things. plus, joanne doesn't come home for breakfast after seminary any more. she just goes straight to school. it's strange, but in spite of everything i really care about joanne, and i'm worried about her. i guess we've been through a lot together, one way or another, and i really know how she feels. i do. if only she would let me tell her.

as for cam, i don't know what to do with him. he won't let me in. his face is closed to me. i think he's mad at me too for some reason. maybe he thinks i'm somehow an accomplice in all the crimes against him because of how i feel for joanne and because i just want to forget this whole mess and get back to how things were before.

today when we sat in the library during our free period he actually studied and didn't interrupt me once. when i tried to joke with him, he just glared at me. "what did i do?" i asked, to which he said "i need to study, okay." so i said "fine, i'll leave you to it then." and i packed up my stuff and walked away. of course i wanted him to follow me, and we'd both apologize and talk and get things into the open and everything would be okay again. but he didn't follow me, so now neither of us knows where we stand with each other.

i think i might have to leave cam to horace and leona. obviously i'm not getting through to him but maybe they can. maybe things will get better when our two week sentence is up. only a week and a bit left, but it's going to be a long week. actually, i think cam is more confused than angry. maybe he just needs time to work things out in his own mind. whatever is going on i hope it ends soon.

oh well. there's not a lot i can do right now so i guess i'll go to bed.

goodnight.

_____ _Seventeen_

Novi talked to Horace and Leona the next day in the cafeteria. Cam was late coming from his last morning class, so Novi used the time to discuss the problem with her friends.

"I don't know what to do," Novi said.

"Well, what exactly is the problem?" Leona asked.

"He's so angry. And he's closed himself off. He's shut me out completely. But I don't know why he's mad at me."

Horace tipped his chair back and looked at the ceiling. He always did this before he said something wise or deep. Leona and Novi smiled at each other, because even though Horace was usually right he was always so theatrical with his little speeches.

"It seems to me," Horace began slowly.

"Yes, yes?" Leona and Novi asked eagerly, trying to bug Horace. He just scowled at them and continued.

"It seems to me that Cam is angry for several reasons. He's mad because he got beat up. But I think he's mad at you, Novi, because deep down he knows you're right; that he should just let it go. He's also mad because the right thing to do is forgive and forget, but he wants some kind of justice and that's not going to happen, and that's not fair, so he's mad."

"What?" Leona teased.

"I don't get it," Novi said.

"You guys are just jealous," Horace said, as he took a sandwich out of his lunch bag and started to eat.

"No, Horace, listen," Novi said, serious again. "I know why Cam is mad. I need to know what to do about it. I mean, he's put me in an awful position. He basically told me that if I'm nice to my cousin, then he's not my friend anymore."

"Really?" Horace asked. "He said that?"

"In so many words."

"Well, I see his point," Leona said. "Your cousin didn't beat him up herself but she might as well have."

"But she feels so bad," Novi argued. "And I think she's out of the gang now. I mean, she's wandering the halls of this school all alone, with no one to protect her from Buffy."

"No, not Buffy," Horace screeched. And they all went into a no-not-Buffy attack, screeching and cowering and hitting each other across the table. Most of their conversations collapsed into this kind of chaos in the end.

They were still acting silly when Cam came up to the table and flopped down in his chair. He mumbled hello and started eating his lunch.

The gang tried to become serious in honor of Cam's mood. Novi cast a meaningful glance at Horace to get him to talk to Cam about the situation.

"Cam, this is the fifth lunch-time frivolity you've spent in silence," Horace said in his best adult voice.

"Yeah. So?" Cam said, challenging.

"So, you're starting to bring us down," Leona said. Novi winced.

"Do you want me to leave?" Cam demanded, rising, ready to grab his stuff and go.

Horace stood up and put his hands on Cam's shoulders, gently pushing him back into his chair. "Cam, we're just trying to lighten things up, okay?"

"Well, don't bother."

"Cam, how long is this going to go on?" Novi finally said, exasperated. "We're your friends. Why are you treating us this way?"

"You don't know how I feel," Cam said, looking at the table.

"Well, tell us, then," Horace said.

"Talk, baby, talk," Leona prompted. Novi just looked at Cam imploringly.

Cam looked up from the table at his three friends. He was trying to decide whether to be angry at them for ganging up on him or to be grateful to them for being his friends.

"Just give me one good reason why I shouldn't be angry anymore."

"Because you're not happy hanging on to this stupid thing," Novi said.

"Because it isn't hurting anyone but yourself," Horace said. "I mean, Doug and Todd are probably loving it that you're so upset about the whole thing."

"Because," Leona added, "we like you a lot better when you're happy."

"I only asked for one reason," Cam said, trying not to laugh. This made everyone else laugh with relief. Novi was so relieved that she stood up and gave Cam a big kiss. Cam was so surprised and overjoyed that there was no way he could stay mad anymore.

It had been a long, long week for Joanne. So long, in fact, that when Friday morning's classes ended she went to her new locker in the automotives section of the school—the most remote hallway she could find—got her coat and her books, and left.

Instead of walking straight home she went to the ravine and sat down on the bench there. It was getting less cold as February wore on, but even if it had been freezing she wouldn't have cared. Feeling cold took her mind off feeling wretched.

After the fight, on Friday night Joanne had felt so awful that she didn't know whether she could stand it. She felt sick about all she had done, or at least all she had allowed her friends to do; about her spinelessness and her lies. She was disgusted at her insecurity, at her dependence on her friends. She was horrified at all the time she had wasted with those people, and at what she was quickly realizing she had become while she was with them: a frightened, personality-less liar, too afraid to do the right thing.

Then, on Sunday, everything had fallen apart inside her. She had cried for hours; her sobs would subside, then she would think of some other thing that was wrong with her and her life and the crying would begin again. She cried through supper, staying in her room, just lying on her bed. She cried all evening, finally falling asleep around ten-thirty, exhausted from the effort and exhausted by her tortured thoughts.

On Monday she had got up early as usual, gone to seminary, and then gone straight to the school and moved her things to another locker. The automotives hallway was dark and isolated, and that was exactly how she felt, so it was a perfect place to be.

That Monday had been possibly the worst day of all. Joanne had never felt so utterly lonely in her life. It was an actual physical pain—she felt so remote and distant from the hundreds of people who passed by her in the halls and who sat with her in class. Every cluster of friends, every laugh that rose and fell in the noisy hallways, reminded her that she didn't really know anyone, and even worse, that no one really knew her.

Gradually the aching in the center began to subside, and a kind of numbness set in. Everything became difficult for her; she felt listless and weary, as if she had been walking for days without rest. In a strange way the new numb, lifeless feeling was hardest to take because there seemed no escape from it. It seeped into every breath, every step, every movement, every thought.

So she sat on the bench at the top of the ravine because she just couldn't muster the energy to move; she could find no answer to the question "Why should I move?" so she didn't. If she got up and went home she'd just have to explain to her mother why she wasn't in school, and she had nowhere else to go. She thought about the tingling cold that started to take over her toes and fingers. And when she started to shiver she pulled her knees to her chest and wrapped her arms tightly around them, trying to become the smallest bundle she could be.

After an hour Joanne's ears began to burn with cold, despite her earmuffs. She decided that she didn't really want frostbite, so she got up and slowly walked home.

"Larry?" Trish called from the kitchen when Joanne came in the front door.

"No." Joanne took off her boots and coat and put them away in the front closet.

Trish walked into the front hallway. "Joanne, honey, you're home early. What's wrong?"

"I'm not feeling well, so I left before my last class," Joanne said, not caring that she lied. "So I'm just going to go to bed. If I don't come down for dinner just leave me sleeping, okay?"

Trish walked toward her daughter to put her arm around Joanne's shoulders, but before she could do so Joanne moved away and started up the stairs.

"Joanne," Trish said, concern in her voice. Joanne turned to look at her mother. "Why don't you come into the kitchen and talk? I'll make some hot chocolate."

"No, thanks."

"Honey, don't just sit in your room alone. Why don't you talk to me?"

"Mom, I don't need to talk. I'm sick. I just need to sleep."

With that, Joanne turned away and walked upstairs to her room. She dumped her knapsack in a corner and changed into sweats. Then she crawled under her quilts and curled up as tight as she could. All she wanted to do was sleep. In fact, she couldn't imagine doing anything else at this point. She tried to but couldn't. Sleep was all she wanted, all she could do. So she did.

Trish went back into the kitchen after Joanne went upstairs. She sat down at the kitchen table, where she had been working on a Relief Society lesson for the following Sunday. For half an hour she tried to work but, knowing that Joanne was alone in her dark room, she couldn't concentrate. She thought of phoning her husband, but they had talked about Joanne just about every night this week, and there was really nothing more to say. They were worried, they wanted their daughter to be happy, but as long as she refused their comfort and resisted their help there was nothing they could do.

Trish hated the sense of failure and helplessness she felt. The situation with Joanne made her realize that no matter how hard she tried she couldn't guarantee happiness for her children. She wanted to go and hold Joanne as she had when Joanne was a child. She wanted to keep her two children beside her always so as to protect them from the world, from the cruelties that other people inflicted on each other. She would do anything for her children, but right now, for Joanne, it seemed she could do nothing at all.

So she closed up her Relief Society books and went to the basement, where she was refinishing an old cabinet. She sanded with all her might, using sandpaper instead of the power sander, shutting off her mind and focusing on the rhythmic physical labour, stripping away the cracked, discolored varnish, leaving clean, smooth wood behind the movement of her hands. Here at least she had some power to heal.

Novi came home right after school, this particular requirement being part of her grounding punishment. As she was taking off her outside clothing in the back entranceway, Trish came up from the basement. "Hi Novi," she said. "How was your day?"

"Good," Novi said. "Cam's finally starting to get back to normal. He actually laughed today."

Novi and her aunt walked to the kitchen, where Novi looked in the cupboards for something to eat, finally settling on a banana from the fruit bowl on the table.

"Novi, can I ask you a favor?" Trish said after Novi had hoisted herself up onto the counter beside the sink.

"Sure."

"You might not want to do it, and I'll understand."

"What is it?"

"Well . . ." Trish hesitated, not sure whether she should ask what she was about to ask. Novi seemed fine – despite having been a little subdued this week, she appeared to have recovered from the weekend's crisis. So Trish continued. "I was wondering if you could try talking to Joanne."

Novi laughed.

"I know you're mad at her – "

"No, that's not it," Novi interrupted. "It's just that it's highly unlikely that Joanne will let me talk to her."

"What do you mean?"

"If you haven't noticed, she's been making herself kind of scarce lately. She moved her locker at school away from her friends. I don't know where it is now."

"I didn't know."

"Yeah," Novi continued. "At first I was too mad. There was no way I was going to let Joanne forget how rotten she'd been. But now, well, I'm just worried about her. All along, you know, since I told her she could stick with her friends and not worry about me, I knew how miserable she was. She knew it was wrong, she hated doing it, but she honestly thought she would never get any more friends. I guess you don't just decide one day to get rid of your friends, no matter what they're doing. It's not that easy."

"You're right. It's not that easy." Trish thought for a moment. "Poor Joanne. It sounds like with her old friends you're either for them or against them, and if you're against them, you're in trouble."

"Yup," Novi said shaking her head. "Some friends! How did Joanne get mixed up with them in the first place? She's just not like that."

"Well, I don't think they were always this bad. I think popularity just went to their heads. Besides that, Joanne just wants to belong."

"Teenagers! We're so stupid sometimes," Novi said as she jumped down from the counter and threw the banana peel away. "I mean, most of the time people hate the popular group, because they're usually kind of treacherous, you know? But everyone is nice to them anyway, because they don't want to get in their bad books."

Novi talked as she got some milk from the fridge and poured herself a glassful. "My dream is for my little gang to become the popular group, and we'll be nice to everybody so that no one has to worry or be in competition and everyone will be nice to everyone else." Novi laughed. "Great little fantasy, but there's not a big chance of that happening. People can't seem to get past my haircut when I try to be friendly."

Trish laughed as she surveyed her niece standing in the middle of the kitchen. "Well, my sister must have done something right," she said.

"What do you mean?"

"She's got a pretty amazing daughter."

Novi blushed and did a little bow.

"I just wish Joanne could see things with your perspective. Looking back, I can see that Joanne hasn't really been happy for a while. She had other friends, but at the beginning of last year she sort of took up with these other kids exclusively, and since then, well, I guess she must have felt pretty desperate all the time, always having to watch her back. It's no way to live."

112

Trish wondered how she might have taught Joanne the things Novi already knew. She wondered if it was anything she had done or hadn't done that made Joanne feel so insecure and unsure of herself. She wondered why people made it so hard for each other and themselves. She wondered why things never change, because it had been exactly the same when she went to high school.

"Poor Jo," she finally said, after she had sat quietly for a minute.

"I'll keep trying to talk to her," Novi said as she got her books from the back hallway. "Because, I don't know why, but I like Joanne."

Her aunt looked at her in mock surprise.

"Oh!" Novi said, embarrassed again. "That didn't come out right. You know what I mean."

"Yes, I do," Trish laughed, and she got up from the table and gave Novi a big hug.

Novi was surprised, but she let her do that for a while, pretending in the back of her mind that it was her own mother who held her. Then Novi practically ran from the room, because for some reason she felt that she was going to cry.

When Cam got home from school his mother asked him if he would shovel the driveway for her. His first reaction was to complain, but he checked himself. "No problem, Mom," he said, trying to speak without sarcasm. There wasn't really that much snow to clear, anyway, he reasoned as he put some extra socks and long underwear on beneath his clothing, and donned a toque and some thick-lined leather gloves from the front hall closet.

The cold air and the snow outside somehow made the world seem clean and pure. And silent also. The only sound was that of the shovel scraping the driveway, and even that noise was muted, as if winter had left a film of quiet on everything. Cam's body settled into a rhythm of movement: push the shovel through the snow, and with the momentum of pushing heave the gathered snow onto the growing bank beside the driveway. Take five steps backwards and one to the side, then push the shovel through the snow . . . And so on, until one half of the driveway is cleared. Then do the same until the other half is cleared.

At the foot of the driveway, after tossing the last shovelful of snow onto the drift, Cam stood up straight and stretched his arms back to loosen his shoulder muscles. While working, his whole body focused on the task at hand, Cam had felt the stillness of winter seeping into his mind. He could feel the last remnants of anger and bitterness flowing out of him and becoming lost in the white and frozen world. Standing at the foot of the driveway, he leaned his head back and surveyed the sky right above him, a laden white sky waiting to fill the world with the perfection of snowfall.

Inside the house, Cam's mother hummed a song and set the table for dinner.

_____ _Eighteen_

When Joanne woke up it was dark outside. The clock on her bed table said it was eight o'clock. She was momentarily disoriented, as she usually was when she slept during the day, but the sounds of her family reminded her of where she was. All the thoughts that sleep had let her escape from came flooding back in again, and any healing the nap may have brought seemed destroyed.

Then the sound of Scott laughing rose through the floor and stabbed her in the heart. She didn't know of her parents' concern, or of Novi's. She only knew that they were all downstairs enjoying each other and that even if she wanted to she couldn't join them. She felt as if her separation from everyone was vast and irreparable. _I would be a ghost,_ she thought. _I'd walk into the kitchen where they are laughing together and they wouldn't be able to see me._

Sitting up in her bed, her knees to her chest and her head to her knees, Joanne felt as if she had to hold herself tightly or else she might come apart. She had never felt such all-encompassing loneliness in her life. She was sure she would die from the pain of it. From somewhere under this terrible weight Joanne called out to God for help. She tried to send to her Father the sadness she felt, in hope that he would know that she was buried beneath the darkness and that he would come for her.

Then, as suddenly as the searing dark pain had descended on her at the sound of her brother's laughter, her mind was filled with light. Behind her closed eyes she could see or think of nothing but this white and living light. Tears streamed down her cheeks—tears with sobs, cleansing tears—and her body relaxed. The white light was all around her, all through her, and she could no longer feel or remember the dark room she sat in.

And with the peace that filled her it was as if from out of the light came embracing arms of light. Her mind spoke the word *Father* and, while seconds ago she had felt the blackest weight upon her, wrapped now in peace she felt her body emptied of darkness and pain. The light slowly faded into a velvety blackness, and Joanne was aware of the bed beneath her again. She lay curled on her side like a small child, and tears still streamed down her cheeks. No words came to her mind; it was for the moment perfectly clear. Every muscle in her body tingled as if she had just soaked in hot water. Mind clear, and body healed, Joanne slept again, a long and dreamless sleep.

_____ Nineteen

Of course, no one did anything that weekend, since they were grounded. Novi sneaked a phone call to Cam on Saturday afternoon, when Cam had said his parents would be out.

"How's your lonely weekend going?" Novi asked.

"Oh, it's not so bad. I've been ignoring school a bit lately, so it's good to actually study for once."

"But what I want to know," Novi asked, "is do you miss me terribly?"

"Oh, Novi, my darling, being apart from you is unbearable."

"Okay, good. I just wanted to make sure."

Cam laughed.

"Cam, I've got to go, but I need to ask you something."

"What?"

"Don't be mad, okay?"

"What is it, Novi?" Cam asked impatiently.

"It's Joanne," Novi said, unsure about going on.

"Yes?" Cam waited. "Get to the point, Novi."

"Well, are you still mad at her?"

Cam was silent for a moment. "Um . . . no," he finally said, thoughtfully. "No, I don't think I am. Last week when I talked to Bishop MacInnes I was too mad to do what he said, but he said I should try to understand why people do things and that will make it easier for me to forgive them.''

"Well, have you?''

"Have I forgiven them? Yeah, I guess. But you know, especially Joanne. She didn't really do anything, and I tried to remember why I was ever in the gang, and I think I can understand how she feels.''

"So you wouldn't be mad if I tried to get her to . . . I don't know . . . eat lunch with us, or something?''

"No, I guess not. Just don't expect me to be best friends with her.''

"But you used to be friends with her, remember?''

"Yeah, I guess. It seems like a long time ago.''

"Okay.'' Novi was rushed. "I've really got to go now. Someone's coming. Don't be too lonely tonight.''

"Okay. See you tomorrow.''

Novi hung up just before Larry came into the family room. "Was that a phone call I heard?'' he asked, pretending to be annoyed.

"Oh, I was phoning time . . . maybe?'' Novi ventured.

"Oh. What time is it?''

"I forget.''

"Oh. Okay, Novi.'' He laughed and left the room.

Novi remained for a minute on the family room floor. She had to smile at her uncle. *He's just a big softie,* she thought. *He's got the backbone to put his foot down, but he doesn't go too far. It's funny how things turn out. My family falls apart, but I find a new family. And the best friends I've had in a long time.* Novi let herself think about Cam—she didn't like to let herself dwell on him that often. She used to wonder if she liked him or if she liked the fact that he liked her, but now she was sure that she liked him. She liked him a lot.

And it wasn't just because he looked cool in his new clothes and hair. He knew how to be funny and spontaneous, and he also knew how to really think about things. They had had so many good discussions together during their free periods and, once in a while, after school when they studied together. There was something different about Cam even from Horace, who was a pretty great person himself. Novi had a vague idea that it had something to do with what Cam did on Sunday, dressed in his suit and tie sitting at the sacrament table. Novi wasn't quite sure what it was, but there was something different and good about Cam.

It was the same with Uncle Larry. Novi tried not to compare her father to her uncle, knowing who would lose out in the comparison. She tried not to compare her mother to aunt Trish for the same reason. *Why did Mom stop going to church?* Novi wondered. *Things might have ended up so differently. We might have had a family like this one.*

"What is it, Novi?" It was Trish. Novi hadn't heard her aunt come into the room. Nor had she realized that she was crying. She wiped her face. Her aunt sat down on the arm of the chesterfield and faced her.

"I was just thinking," Novi said.

"Are you okay?"

"Yeah. I was just thinking about how different your family is from mine. Life is so strange sometimes. I mean, there's some really awful things, and some wonderful things, all mixed together."

"Yup. It's true," Trish said, thinking of Joanne.

Novi thought of Joanne too. *It's funny how things turned out,* she thought. *Even with my family's problems, I think I've turned out all right. At least I feel better about myself than Joanne does.*

"You know," Novi said, letting Trish in on her thoughts, "good things sometimes come from bad things, right? I think Joanne's going to be better than ever. I think this whole mess is just what she needed."

"Maybe," her aunt mused. "Maybe."

"Yeah, she'll be fine," Novi said as she stood up. As she spoke she resolved to get through to Joanne no matter how long it took.

119

As she was leaving the room, Novi remembered what she had wanted to ask Trish. She came back into the room and stood by her aunt, who was still perched on the chesterfield arm. "Trish, can I ask you a question?"

"Sure, hon," Trish said, trying to put Joanne out of her mind for the time being.

"Why did my mom stop going to church? She was a member, I know."

"Yes. She still is." She tried to remember the real reasons for her sister's inactivity. "I guess the most obvious reason was that your father wasn't a member of the Church."

"But that's not the only reason, is it?"

"No." Trish paused. "No. I think your mom felt . . . well, I think she might have felt a lot like Joanne does now — you know, a little insecure, wanting to belong, but feeling sure she never could. She was always a bit rebellious, and I think it might have been because she was so sure she couldn't be what people wanted, or be the kind of person she thought she should be, or thought the Church wanted her to be, so she just didn't try. She gave up before she tried, so that she wouldn't ever fail.

"Thinking back, I think she was sad a lot of the time. Everyone used to bug her about being grumpy, but now that I think of it she was just sad. I don't think she liked being the bad girl of the family, but I think she might have thought it was the only thing she could do well."

Novi had started to cry again as Trish spoke. "That's awful," she said.

"I wish I'd done more for her. I just didn't know what to do, or say, you know? Joanne reminds me of your mother, and I worry. Your mother was like you on the outside, but like Joanne on the inside. Joanne deals with her insecurity by doing everything other people say, and your mom dealt with it by doing anything but what people told her to do."

"Oh, that's so awful," Novi said, weeping for her mother, and for Joanne too, and for herself and her aunt.

Everything seemed so sad all of a sudden. She wondered if there was anything anyone could do for anybody else.

Her aunt put her arm around Novi. "You really love people don't you, Novi?"

"But I feel like I can't do anything for them. I mean, my mom, Joanne . . . what can I do?"

"I know how you feel, honey." They stood together for a minute. "The Lord prepareth a way to accomplish all his works among the children of men," she said, not really speaking to Novi; more like thinking aloud to herself.

"Pardon?" Novi asked.

"Oh, I was just thinking that we'll probably be able to figure something out."

"Why?"

"Well, because we're trying to do the right thing, and so the Lord will help us."

"Is that how it works?"

"Yes, hon," Trish said as she gave Novi a squeeze and they walked from the family room together. "That's how it works. One way or another."

_____ Twenty

Joanne woke up Saturday morning after almost twelve hours of sleep. After such a hellish week she needed that much rest, and last night sleeping was all she cared to do. But in the light of day, Joanne was a little embarrassed about it.

For all that, she lay in bed for a while after she was fully awake, trying to figure out what was going on in her head. She thought of how awful she had felt, and it seemed remote from her. Those feelings were gone now. She remembered the amazing things that had happened to her in her room last night, and she knew that the Lord had heard and healed her.

But even now she didn't feel quite right. Looking back, she realized that she hadn't felt right for a long time, only this was different. It was as if she had spent the time with her former friends—she no longer thought of them as her friends—constructing and living in some kind of building, which became her entire world. Then, during the past week, her world had crashed down around her, and all the people she had shared her world with had fled. Now everything was still. The destruction was over. She felt as if she sat alone amid the rubble of her old life, her old self; a last survivor in a bombed-out city.

With her eyes closed she imagined the debris strewn about her, and she realized what inferior materials she had used, what a false and rickety structure she had built, what a shifting foundation she had put the whole mess on top of. *Of course, it had to fall sometime,* she thought, thinking of all the compromises and lies it had taken to keep the building standing. *Really, it's a good thing this happened.*

In the silent aftermath of everything, now she wasn't sure what to do or where to start. She knew that the person she had tried to be was mixed in with the rubble of her life, and she wasn't quite sure who she was, or how to act. She thought of going downstairs, but she didn't know what she would say to her family; she was embarrassed at the thought of trying to be a different person in front of people who perceived her in a particular way. Trying to change the way she acted, the person she was, was like admitting that she had been wrong before. She had been wrong, but it was hard to admit it to the world. While she knew her family would understand, still it was embarrassing, somehow.

But inside she felt a click of resolve and a sudden rush of purpose. She didn't know why she had tried to build a tall and spacious building to live in, or why she had tried to fill it with people like Buffy and Todd and Doug. All she knew was that now the past seemed remote and forgiven. She saw a clear path stretching out in front of her, surrounded by wide green plains, under clear skies. Her family stood before her, beckoning, smiling at her and waiting for her to join them. Picturing this, Joanne wondered why she would want to look down at the world from a tenth-story window with only Buffy for company when she could walk in the fresh air with people she loved and with heaven waiting in the distance.

_____ Twenty-one

It was just coincidence that Novi was there when it happened. She rarely walked down that particular hallway at school, but today at lunch Leona had mentioned a new painting she was working on, and Novi was on her way to the art room to have a look at it.

Novi saw Joanne and her old gang as soon as she turned the corner. She quickly backed up and peeked around the corner to see what was going on. Joanne and the others were at the far end of the hallway. Novi could clearly see that Buffy had taken Joanne's binder and was ripping all the loose leaf sheets out, one by one, and tossing them on the floor. Novi couldn't hear the exact words Buffy spoke, but she could imagine them from the tone of the mumbles she could hear. Despite all her efforts, Buffy was pretty predictable.

Doug and Todd were leaning against the lockers and laughing. Jill looked a lot like Joanne had always looked whenever Novi had seen her with her friends. There was a new girl with them whom Novi didn't know, but who was obviously Joanne's replacement. The new girl cheered Buffy on, a little too enthusiastically.

Novi watched for a second more, then ran to the art room by another hallway. She spotted Leona, who was at the sink cleaning brushes.

"Leona, quick," Novi said, grabbing Leona's arm. "We've got to save Joanne."

"What are you talking about?" Leona asked, as she quickly dried her hands.

Novi tugged Leona along as she explained. "Okay, as soon as we get up to Joanne, you've got to gather up all the papers from the floor. Just grab them, and then grab Joanne and walk. Don't say anything."

"Okay," Leona shrugged. "Whatever you say, boss."

Novi and Leona stopped just before turning the corner into the hallway where Joanne was in trouble.

"They'll be right there when we turn the corner," Novi whispered.

"Who's they?"

"Buffy and company." Leona nodded, finally understanding. "Okay, let's go."

Novi and Leona strode fearlessly around the corner and walked directly up to Joanne. Leona bent down and quickly gathered the papers together. Novi yanked the binder out of Buffy's hands, looking her steadily in the eye as she did so. Joanne watched in disbelief and stumbled slightly as Novi and Leona each grabbed an arm and pulled her away from Buffy and the others. As she was whisked away she glanced backwards long enough to see the old gang standing there dumbfounded—Jill smiling slightly, and Buffy with her hands frozen in the position they had been in when Novi had seized the binder.

"Mission completed," Novi said with a grin after they had turned the corner and run to safety a few hallways away.

Joanne looked down at the floor as Novi and Leona put the loose papers back in the binder. "Thanks a lot, you guys," she said as Novi handed her book to her. "I don't know what to say."

"I don't know about you," Leona said, "but I thought it was kind of fun. Did you see the look on Buffy's face?"

126

Novi was still grinning. "Yes indeed. That was surely a fulfilling experience. Not that I'm into revenge or anything petty like that. Not at all."

"So are you okay?" Leona asked Joanne. "No bruises or broken bones?"

Joanne winced slightly. Novi gave Leona a dirty look. "No, I'm fine."

"Okay, then," Leona said, walking away. "Back to my masterpiece. See you chicks later."

Novi and Joanne watched Leona walk down the hall and disappear around the corner. Joanne glanced at Novi, then looked at the floor again.

"So what were you doing wandering the halls alone? Are you skipping?"

"No, this is my free period," Joanne said.

"You're kidding. You mean we've had the same free period all along and we didn't know it?"

"I guess."

Novi looked at Joanne standing timidly in front of her more like a frightened child than a seventeen-year-old. She checked her watch, slipped her arm into Joanne's, and started pulling her down the hall.

"Come on, cuz, we've got half an hour left. Just enough time to find your locker and move your stuff to a safe location. Somewhere where I can keep an eye on you."

"No, Novi, I can't. I mean . . . No," Joanne stuttered.

"Listen, Jo, no arguments, please. I just saved your life. You have to do whatever I say."

"Don't get me wrong," Joanne protested. "I'm really grateful, but . . . well, what about your friends?"

"Oh, don't worry, you'll love 'em."

"No, that's not what I mean. They must hate me. I know Cam does."

"They'll get used to you. They got used to me, didn't they?"

Joanne stopped walking and turned to face Novi. "Why are you doing this? I don't understand. After everything I've done. I just don't get it."

"What's there to get?" Novi shrugged. "You're my favorite cousin named Joanne—it's the least I could do." Novi grabbed Joanne's arm again. "All right? So. Where's your locker?"

"The automotives hallway," Joanne said, embarrassed.

"No wonder I couldn't find you," Novi laughed. Joanne laughed too—for the first time in a long time.

"Okay, you guys," Novi instructed her three friends. "She'll be here any minute now. Just be friendly. Act natural."

Horace, Leona, and Cam nodded obediently, smiling and rolling their eyes as soon as Novi turned her back.

"I saw that," she said, whipping around. Everyone laughed.

"I'm going to get in trouble if I don't get home, Nov," Cam said. "We're grounded, remember?"

"She's probably too shy to come, knowing we're all standing here," Horace said. "She'll probably just wait until we're gone."

"So let's get gone," Leona suggested, never having liked the idea of a welcoming committee in the first place.

"Maybe you're right." Novi thought for a minute, her forehead crinkling slightly in concentration. "Okay, here's the plan." (More eye rolling from the friends.) Novi continued, "I'll talk to Joanne and get her to eat lunch with us. And everyone will be nice and friendly. Got it?"

"Yes, sir, Sergeant Kosnowski, sir," Cam said, saluting her. She hit him on the head with her mittens.

"Go away, you losers," she said as her friends waved good-bye.

"*A demain, mon ami,*" Horace shouted as the three of them turned the corner. Novi could hear them talking and laughing as they walked to the exit and left the school.

Just then, Joanne peeked her head around the corner. "Aha! There you are," Novi said. "Yes, they're gone. Come on, hurry up. If we get home late we'll be in trouble."

"Well, go ahead," Joanne said. "You don't have to wait."

"Oh yeah? I bet you don't remember the locker combination."

Joanne blushed. "Oh. Hmm. I guess you're right. Thanks for waiting."

Neither Novi nor Joanne spoke as Joanne got her things from the locker and they left the school. Joanne felt shy and awkward, still stuck in the silence she'd lived in for the past while. And Novi, although overjoyed that she'd been able to get through to Joanne so soon, wasn't sure how Joanne was feeling, or how far she should push this friendship thing. After considering it for a moment, Novi decided that the best way to find out was just to ask.

"So, how are you doing? Are you okay?"

"What do you mean?" Joanne asked, embarrassed. She was feeling embarrassed a lot today.

"Well, you've had a bad week. I was really worried."

"I'm fine. I . . ." Joanne didn't know what to say. She knew it would feel good to talk, but it was too soon.

"You can talk to me, Jo," Novi said seriously. "I've been waiting for two months for you to talk to me."

"I've wanted to talk to you, too," Joanne said quietly. "Can you wait a while longer? I need to figure some things out first."

"Well, I guess. But I'm going to keep bugging you. It would help you figure things out if you'd just talk about it." As Novi said this she grabbed a handful of snow from a drift by the sidewalk. And as emphasis, she plopped it down on Joanne's head.

"Hey!" Joanne yelled, as the snow trickled down her back. "Is violence necessary?" She grabbed a handful of snow and retaliated by stuffing it down the front of Novi's coat. They were soon having a full-fledged snowball fight,

129

which lasted until they were both too tired and too wet to continue.

They walked the rest of the way home slowly, both wanting to savor their time together. Joanne couldn't believe her good fortune. Just days ago she had been imagining a solitary future and was utterly confused about how to rebuild her life. Now, with Novi walking beside her, making her feel completely at ease, the future seemed clearer and a lot less lonely. And whereas just days ago Joanne wasn't sure who she was or how she should act, with Novi she felt that she was exactly herself, and that she knew how to be herself without ever having to think about it.

As for Novi, she was enjoying herself immensely. The fact that Buffy had returned Joanne to her gave her great pleasure. She hoped the irony wasn't lost on Buffy. *My instinct was right all along,* Novi thought. *This is the real Joanne. Maybe she can finally be happy and I can stop feeling guilty for coming here.*

When Joanne and Novi walked in the back door, wet and joking together, Trish thought she must be dreaming. Novi burst into the kitchen and Joanne followed shyly behind.

''What's to eat, auntie dear?'' Novi asked, as she looked through all the cupboards, stopping in front of the fridge and just staring at the food inside.

Trish walked to her daughter and smiled. ''Honey, I'm so glad you're back,'' and she took Joanne in her arms and held her for a long time.

Twenty-two

So the next day Joanne timidly joined Novi and her friends for lunch. This caused quite a stir among cafeteria regulars—to see yet another member of Buffy's gang defecting to "the weird table," as they affectionately called the place where Novi and company sat every day. People wondered what was going on. The mystique and appeal of the small band of rebels began to grow.

During that first lunch Joanne remained silent, only speaking when asked a direct question. But gradually, because everyone was so casual and acted as if it was only natural that she would be eating lunch with them, Joanne began to relax a little. Leona had given up her tiny grudge, Horace had been friendly from the start, and Cam understood better than anyone how Joanne felt and tried to let her know this. Joanne finally felt a sense of belonging, a sense that the people around her wanted her there—something she had never felt with her former friends.

By Friday, Joanne no longer felt like a trespasser, and quiet but happy she sat in the cafeteria working on a chemistry assignment for that afternoon and listening to Horace and Novi discuss what they should do to celebrate the end of the two weeks' grounding while they waited for Cam and Leona to show up.

"I don't want to watch a video," Horace said. Novi agreed.

"Come on, Joanne," Horace prompted. "Let's have some help here."

"We could play Monopoly," Joanne joked, looking up from her homework.

"Very funny," Novi said, as she unpacked her lunch, laying her sandwich and apple in front of her. "Could my lunch possibly be any less appealing?" she mused.

Just then Leona came charging into the cafeteria, waving a piece of paper in the air. Cam followed behind her, laughing at her antics.

"You'll never guess," Leona practically shouted. "I'm in. I got accepted."

"That's great," Horace said, jumping up and throwing his arms around Leona. They started doing a crazy polka together through the cafeteria.

"What's all this about?" Novi asked Cam as they watched Horace and Leona put on their little show.

"From what I could piece together," Cam explained, "she got accepted to an art school in Vancouver."

Everyone congratulated Leona when she and Horace finally made their way back to the table.

"You never said anything about this before," Novi scolded Leona.

"Well, I didn't want to say anything because it would be too embarrassing if I didn't get in."

"That's positive thinking for you," Joanne said.

"What about you guys?" Leona asked, still beaming, physically unable to stop smiling. "Where are you guys going to school?"

Joanne and Cam had both applied to the same university in Edmonton. "We'll get in, I'm sure," Cam said, "but the admission deadline is April the first, so we probably won't hear anything until after that."

Everyone looked at Novi, who hadn't spoken yet. "What about you?" Leona asked.

"I was thinking about going to school back home in Winnipeg," Novi said, "but now I don't know."

"Hey, why don't you go to the U of A?" Cam said. "You and Joanne can be roommates."

"Hey, yeah," Joanne said enthusiastically.

"It's a possibility," Novi said, smiling at Joanne's excitement.

While they ate lunch they talked about their plans for the upcoming year. Horace told them he'd already applied to a university in Vancouver.

"I guess I just can't stand to be away from Leona," he said.

"So how are we going to celebrate my triumph," Leona asked, "and where?"

"Can't be at my house," Cam said as he ate an apple.

"Doesn't your mother like me?" Leona asked, pretending to be injured.

"*Your* mother doesn't like you," Cam retorted. He looked at Horace, who put his hand up for a high five. It was always fulfilling to get Leona at her own game of verbal sparring.

"Very funny. I guess it's the basement again."

"What are we going to do?" Novi asked.

The gang sat in silence for a minute, trying to come up with something to do.

"Bridge?" Cam suggested. Novi shoved him out of his chair.

"Elvis film festival?" Horace suggested. Leona swatted him on the back of the head.

"I've got an idea," Joanne said quietly, while they all looked at her expectantly. "How about Twister?"

"That's it!" Cam shouted.

"Yes, yes, yes!" Horace and Leona said in unison.

Cam grabbed Novi's hand and pulled her away from the table. They went into a contorted twister position. Horace grabbed Leona and Joanne and they added themselves to the pile. Then they each reached out and yanked someone away from a neighboring table and soon there was a huge dot-less twister-fest going on. It would have grown, too, if the supervising teacher hadn't come along to ruin everything. Although tickling had threatened to topple the whole affair anyway.

Short-lived as it was, the little twister display had the entire cafeteria, including the supervising teacher, grinning for the rest of the lunch hour.

Well, almost the entire cafeteria. One girl, standing in line to pay for her french fries, witnessed the scene with disgust. As she shoved her money at the cafeteria lady, Buffy decided that this was the last straw. First Novi and Leona humiliate her in front of her friends, and now these misfits were trying to turn her school into Woodstock or something. Well, the rain had fallen on Woodstock, and Buffy was determined to rain on this little party too.

The fun of Twister only lasted about forty-five minutes. After that the gang sat together on the floor singing songs, or listening to Horace play some of his own compositions on the guitar. Eventually Leona put a record on, and they talked while they munched the food they had brought.

"I think you guys should come visit us in Vancouver," Horace said. "During reading week or something."

"You think we're made of money?" Novi asked, as she crunched on chips.

Cam cleared his throat. "Uh, actually, to be honest, I'm not completely sure if I'm going to school next year."

"What?" everyone shouted.

"Why not?" Novi demanded. "Aren't your marks good enough? I could help you study. I thought you said you'd already applied."

"My marks are okay and, yes, I did apply, but I might have to work so I can go on my mission. I'm not sure if my parents can pay for the whole thing. My sister's at BYU and my dad's helping my brother pay back his student loans, so, I mean, there's not a lot of money floating around.''

"Yeah, I've heard about you Mormons and your weird rituals,'' Leona said as she got up to pour herself another glass of pop.

Cam looked at Joanne, who smiled and gave him the thumbs-up sign.

"You never said anything about this before,'' Novi said, seriously. ''I mean, I thought . . . well, I don't know what I thought.''

Cam got on his knees, clasped his hands in front of him, and looked imploringly at Novi. ''Will you wait for me while I'm on my mission, Novi? Will you write me every week and not talk to any other boy the whole time I'm gone? Will you be waiting at the airport when I return? Then, will you marry me?''

Joanne was crying, she was laughing so hard.

"What's so funny?'' Leona asked her.

"I guess you had to be there,'' Joanne sputtered.

Novi pushed Cam over, almost knocking him into the chip dip.

"You know, that's a good idea,'' Horace said. ''Leona, do you want to get married?''

She thought for a second. ''That's a good idea. Sure. We're always together, anyway. How many kids do you want?''

"Oh, can't you imagine a whole gaggle of little Leonas and Horaces?''

"It's perfect. Let's go tell my parents.''

Horace and Leona ran up the stairs laughing. The others didn't know whether to believe them or not.

The group ended up going to a playground and playing tag, jumping from one playground fixture to another and trying not to touch the ground. Joanne turned out to be the most agile, and she wasn't ''it'' once. Horace kept overjumping and landing on the ground instead of on the wooden logs that stuck out from the snow and that they were using as stepping stones. He blamed it on poor depth perception. Everyone else blamed it on lack of coordination.

A little before midnight the party broke up and the teenagers said their good-byes and went home, ready for an extra pair of socks or a tub of hot water to try and thaw out their frozen toes.

"How about some hot chocolate?" Joanne said, as she and Novi took off their boots and coats in the front hallway.

"Good idea. I'll tell your parents we're home."

Ten minutes later the two girls sat at the kitchen table dressed in nightgowns, sweatshirts, and big woolen socks, sipping on steaming hot chocolate.

"Joanne, what is this mission thing?" Novi asked, rubbing her hands on the warm hot-chocolate mug.

"Well, in our church guys go on missions when they turn nineteen. Girls can go when they're twenty-one. They get their call to wherever—it could be anywhere in the world—and they go for two years."

"What do they do?"

"They teach people the gospel."

"Oh yeah? You mean like missionaries taught the Indians?" Novi asked suspiciously. "Do they teach people how bad their cultures are too?"

"No," Joanne explained. "Missionaries learn the language, and learn about the culture of wherever they're going. I know what you mean, but I think missionaries are given pretty strict instructions about respecting people's cultures."

"Well, that's good."

Novi sat for a minute, staring at the table in thought. "Does everyone have to go on a mission?"

"Well, I guess no one has to do anything. But it is a commandment, if that's what you mean."

"Whoa! A commandment. Sounds serious. But you don't have to do it?"

"No one is forcing anyone to do anything." Joanne spoke slowly, trying to choose the right words and trying to figure out what she really meant to say. "Everyone has their free agency, so we can do whatever we want. No one has to go on a mission, no one has to not smoke, or whatever."

"So why does anyone ever do these things?"

"Because . . ." Joanne paused. "Because they believe it's the right thing. Initially, that might not be the reason, but if it's going to last, or be real, that has to be the reason."

"Do you believe?" Novi asked. She was watching Joanne carefully.

"Yes."

"But how do you know? I mean, how do you know it's the right thing?" Novi asked earnestly.

"Well, from personal experience I know how miserable I feel when I do the wrong thing." Joanne shook her head and smiled ruefully, thinking about all the time she had wasted with Buffy. She looked at Novi, who was listening attentively. Joanne leaned forward. "Listen, Novi. After Cam got beat up, oh, man. Was I in bad shape. I just . . . well, I just didn't know what to do. I felt so alone. That sounds like a cliché, but that's how I felt. Utterly isolated. It was awful." Joanne sipped her hot chocolate and looked into space for a second, collecting her thoughts.

"All I could think of to do was pray, you know? So I kind of moaned this pitiful little prayer, like, 'Heavenly Father, please help me.' That's all I said," The two girls looked at each other intently now. "I don't know how to describe it, but one second everything was dark and I felt like the whole world was dragging me down; then the next second, every-thing was light, and all the heaviness was gone. It was like . . . well, I felt like Heavenly Father just forgave me, and all I felt was this peace."

Tears were running down Joanne's cheeks. Novi could feel tears forming in her own eyes. "Why am I crying?" she asked.

Joanne smiled. "How you're feeling right now, that's how you know if things are right."

Novi nodded, beginning to understand. Joanne continued. "I pray for help, and three days later you save me from Buffy and I've got a whole new set of friends. Real friends. Just because I made a few right decisions. That's how I know that what I believe is the right thing. How I feel now as I'm telling you—that's how I know."

Novi looked at her hot chocolate mug for a moment, running her finger slowly around the rim. "It's funny, you know," she said softly. "Sometimes I feel like I'm the old one, the one who has to help you and Cam get your lives together." She smiled at Joanne as she said this. "But when I talk to you guys about your beliefs, like right now, or when I'm with your family, I feel just like a little kid. It's like I'm this little kid learning how to read, or something, and thinking how great it is and feeling like I've got this incredible new power and just wanting to learn more and more. You know?"

"Yeah. I know."

For some time the two girls sat at the kitchen table without speaking. It was unnecessary. They understood completely. Finally, Joanne got up and took the empty mugs to the sink. Novi stood up too, and they walked upstairs together, arm in arm, in silence.

Twenty-three

Novi, Cam, Joanne, and Horace raced after Leona.
"What's going on?" they shouted to her as she ran ahead.
"Just hurry up!" she yelled. She stormed through the halls and out of the school into the parking lot. As soon as the others saw Leona's car they understood what was wrong.
"Oh, my goodness," Joanne moaned.
"Buffy," Novi said. The others just nodded.
Leona's car was a mess. Eggs—about two dozen of them—had been smashed on practically every square inch of the car, and they were now frozen stuck onto the cold metal. The windows were covered with toothpaste. Leona tried to open the passenger door, but someone had poured water in the lock and down the side. She tried the other door, and it was frozen shut also.
They just stood there staring at the car, completely dumbfounded. It would take hours to get it clean.
"Look at that tire," Horace whispered. They hadn't noticed before, but one of the tires had been slashed.
"Oh, my goodness," Joanne moaned again, feeling guilty all over again because of her past associations.
Leona was too upset to speak.
"I can't believe it," Novi gasped.

"I can," Cam said, the anger he had tried so hard to get rid of rising in his throat again. "Those guys . . ." He didn't finish.

Horace went to Leona and put his arm around her. She turned to him, hid her face against his coat, and started to cry.

After the initial shock, the gang planned an emergency meeting for after school. Novi and Joanne headed to the office, leaving the two boys with Leona to prevent her from doing anything rash.

This new crime had a powerful effect on Joanne. It vividly brought back to her the sordid past — her life with Buffy — and that was a time Joanne did not want to be reminded of. She felt a strong need rising up in her to do something to make up for her own past sins of complicity, and this latest prank was just what she needed to prod her into action. It was not enough to quit hanging out with Buffy, Joanne thought. She had to stop her. Joanne didn't know how, but she knew she had to do it. Glancing at Novi beside her as they rushed together to the office, Joanne felt herself grow bolder, vowing that this time she wasn't going to be a victim, or a coward.

"I've been keeping my eye on all of you," Mrs. Fletcher said to Novi and Joanne after returning to her office from the parking lot, where she had examined Leona's car. "I'm aware of the situation with Buffy. I think you're right; it was probably them."

"It was them," Joanne interrupted. "I know it."

"But," Mrs. Fletcher continued, "if they deny it, which they will, it will be your word against theirs, and they'll be innocent until proven guilty."

"Someone must have seen them. I mean, you've got to do something about this," Novi pleaded.

"We'll do some detective work. I want whoever did this to be punished. This cannot be allowed to happen."

"Did you know they beat Cam up?" Joanne said. "I know them. They did it."

"I'll do what I can."

Mrs. Fletcher did call in all the members of Buffy's gang, and they did deny any part in the vandalizing of Leona's car. Mrs. Fletcher promised Leona she would keep looking into the matter, but the group knew that a less official and perhaps more effective response had to be made. So after school they gathered in the remote automotives hallway where Joanne once had had her locker.

"I thought this was finished," Leona said.

"Buffy is incredible," Novi said with disgust. "You know, this happened because we embarrassed her that day, Leona."

"Well, what are we going to do about it?" Cam demanded. Horace was about to speak, but Cam cut him off. "I don't want to hear about your pacifist ideas, Horace."

"What do you want to do, slash their tires?" Horace countered.

"That's exactly what I'd like to do." But Cam knew Horace was right. Everyone did. However, they also were firmly convinced that something had to be done. They just couldn't think of what.

Joanne, who had been wandering up and down the hall deep in thought, opening and closing all the empty lockers as she walked, suddenly stopped and mumbled something to herself. She had been trying all afternoon to come up with a plan to stop Buffy and now she had it.

"What?" Novi asked. "What did you say?"

Joanne turned to them, her face alight with excitement. " 'Love your enemies,' " she recited. " 'Bless them that curse you, do good to them that hate you.' I knew seminary had to be good for something," Joanne laughed. " 'Do good to them that hate you.' "

"What's your point?" Leona said impatiently.

"Wait," Horace said, turning Joanne's idea over in his mind. "I like it. In fact, I love it. Where did you come up with that?"

"It's in the Bible, Horace," Cam scolded.

Novi thought about the idea too. "I'm afraid I don't quite get it."

"Neither do I," Leona grumped.

"Well," Joanne explained, "we pay back their little pranks with love. I mean, we drown them with love. We bake them cookies, we smile at them in the hall, we give them presents. They vandalize our car, we clean theirs. We'll be so nice to them that they'll have to leave us alone just to get us off their backs."

"That's fabulous!" Horace beamed, running up to Joanne and hugging her.

"There's no way that will work," Leona argued.

"I'm a little skeptical myself," Cam admitted.

"Can you think of anything better?" Novi asked.

Leona and Cam shook their heads.

"Okay, then," Novi decided. "Let's try it."

"The love solution," Joanne said.

"The love solution," the others repeated after her.

Novi got a piece of paper from her knapsack and the five teenagers set about planning how to smother their enemies with kindness.

Twenty-four

The love solution was implemented immediately, and soon everyone, even Leona and Cam, was caught up in it. It might have been the wonderful, shocked looks they got when they asked Todd, with extreme sincerity, how he was doing; or when they bought french fries for everyone at Buffy's table one lunch hour; or when they simply waved and shouted hello to members of the other gang in the hallway. Whatever it was that made it so, the love solution was fun, and it seemed to be working.

In fact, Joanne was worried that maybe it was working too well. "Look at them," she whispered to Novi one lunch hour as Buffy and her friends entered the cafeteria. They were trying to look defiant and unconcerned, but Jill kept casting furtive glances Joanne's way, with a pleading look on her face to please not be nice to them this lunch hour. Doug and Todd didn't look anyone in the eye as they walked directly to their table and sat down with their backs turned to the rest of the cafeteria. Buffy seemed as cool and sly as ever, but she didn't say a word to anyone as she moved past the tables to her own; and, like the boys, she sat so that Joanne and her friends were to her back.

"What's wrong with them?" Novi asked. "Except that they're not bugging anyone. Thankfully."

"I don't know," Joanne shrugged. "It just seems like we're humiliating them."

As if to prove Joanne's point, someone shouted to Buffy's table: "Hey, isn't it anyone's birthday today?" To which the people at the surrounding tables laughed gleefully. The day before had been Doug's birthday, so at lunch the rebels had honored him with a soulful rendition of "Happy Birthday," as well as with a beautiful chocolate cake. Not only that, but they had also decorated all the other gang members' lockers with balloons and streamers and signs saying things like "Peace," "Love," and "Have a groovy day."

"Hey, Buffy. Peace," someone shouted, and there was another round of mocking laughter.

"See what I mean?" Joanne said. "They're a laughing stock. I think we'd better stop. I mean, this has served its purpose. We're just embarrassing them now."

"Yeah." Leona grinned. "Don't you love it?"

"But I don't think we're supposed to do good to those who hate us so we can humiliate them."

"I agree," Horace said. "I think we've made our point."

"We're just as bad as they are if we keep it up," Joanne said. Thinking about this, the others had to agree, and it was reluctantly decided to discontinue the rather sweet revenge.

"We have to do the air guitar thing, though," Cam insisted. "That's just too good to pass up."

"Can we still be nice to people too?" Novi asked Joanne, teasing her. "If we keep this up we could change the world. People would start to like each other. They'd smile, say hi, be friendly, you know? We could start a revolution."

"The love revolution," Horace said. "Sounds like a song." He got a little notebook from his back pocket and wrote down his idea.

"So when do we rehearse?" Leona asked. They had decided that at the annual air guitar contest that Friday they would perform a special song dedicated to Buffy and her gang. It was going to be the grand finale of their plan.

"How about the basement Wednesday and Thursday?" Novi suggested. "This has got to be perfect."

Everyone agreed. Laughing, they touched milk cartons, and drank a toast to love.

The next day Horace came to school with a new idea for the air guitar contest. The gang loved it, even though it was going to take a lot of work, and they rehearsed every day that week in preparation. By Friday they were ready.

Cam had bribed some student union official to place the gang as the last act in the show, since they wanted their number to be the big finish. Now, practically the whole school sat in the auditorium, caught up in the excitement of actually having fun during school time, and since up to the previous number none of the acts had shown much imagination or polish, the noisy audience was ready and anxious for a really good act—which was what they were expecting from Novi and her friends.

In fact, the crowd of teenagers cheered when the MC announced that the next act would be "The Weirdos." Everyone knew who that was.

"They love us already." Leona beamed backstage.

As for Joanne, she felt as if she was a little girl again, performing with Novi on the front lawn. Only this time she wasn't embarrassed or ashamed. A little nervous maybe, but overjoyed. She looked at Novi just as Novi had been trying to catch her eye, and the girls grinned at each other.

"Ready?" Horace asked.

Everyone nodded.

"Let's blow them away."

They let out a gleeful whoop and walked on stage. They were dressed in hippie style: replete with love beads, fringes, flowers, round sunglasses, and various other 'sixties-type memorabilia. Horace carried his guitar, the others pushed

145

onto the stage the auditorium piano, at which Joanne sat down when it was in place. Then the others each took an instrument from the top of the piano—Cam, a tambourine; Novi, a set of bongos; and Leona, a recorder—and prepared to play.

Horace began by strumming his guitar. He gave the four count and the others joined in. Then Horace started to sing.

> This is the love solution.
> We're starting a love revolution.
> You can slap us,
> But we're going to turn the other cheek.
> You can hate us,
> But in the end
> Love is strong and hate is weak.
> This is the love solution.
> We're starting a love revolution.

The others sang three-part harmony on the chorus, then each took a turn on the verses. By the end of the song the whole audience was singing along with them. They repeated the chorus several times before Horace gave another four count, and the song ended. The practice had paid off because "The Weirdos" almost sounded like a real band, and "Love Revolution" was a great song, upbeat and catchy.

The audience went wild when the song was over. Five stars had been born. All afternoon, people ran up to members of the gang to congratulate them, tell them how great the song was, ask for a tape of the song, or just slap them on the back and grin. The grins came about because people knew who the song had been for, and they knew that Buffy and her friends had been deposed. They were no longer a threat or even an interest to the previously intimidated school population. Someone had finally shown enough courage to tell the emperor about his new clothes.

After school the gang stood around by their lockers discussing their triumph. None of them could stop smiling. Even their teachers had congratulated them on their performance.

"I really like this celebrity thing," Cam said.

"Yeah, me too," Leona agreed. "I can't believe it. People are treating us like rock stars."

"I think we should start a real band," Novi said.

Joanne laughed. "Are you kidding? Horace is the only one with any talent."

Horace smirked, and took a bow.

"That's not true," the others yelled.

"I play a mean recorder solo," Leona argued.

"And did you hear those harmonies?" Novi demanded.

"No thanks to you, Miss Tone-deaf," Cam teased.

"I am not."

"Oh, no. We're fighting." Horace cringed. "Does this mean that the band is breaking up? No!"

"How will the rock world survive?"

"No, really," Leona interrupted. "Someone from student council asked if we'd consider playing a few songs at Grad."

"You're kidding."

"Honest."

They were still talking about the future possibilities of fame and fortune as they put their coats on, getting ready to go to the local fast-food joint for an after-school celebration, when Buffy, followed by Jill, Todd, and Doug, came down the hallway. The girl who had replaced Joanne was gone, probably having fled the group as soon as their fall from grace began.

The gang stopped talking and stood still as Buffy approached.

"Quite a performance," she said.

"Thanks."

"Hi Joanne. Cam." They both nodded.

Buffy looked heavenward for a moment. "So, what are you guys trying to prove? What's your point?"

147

"We don't have anything to prove," Novi said.

"What's your point, then?" Todd glared.

"You know, I could really ask you the same," Horace began calmly. "I mean, it seems to me that it was you guys that were out to prove something. We just wanted to get rid of you. I guess our point is that you can't intimidate us. We don't think your methods will work in the long run. You can have power or you can have friendship. You can't have both."

Joanne stepped forward and looked Buffy steadily in the eye. She was about to speak but she changed her mind, and shaking her head she turned away from Buffy and moved beside Novi.

Buffy laughed unconvincingly. "Well, if you've had your fun, kids, do you think you could give me a big break and just get out of my life?"

The gang looked at each other. "What do you think?" Cam asked.

"I don't know. What do you think?" Leona teased.

"I guess we could do that. Happy to be of service to you, Buffy." Novi grinned.

Buffy turned to leave. "Come on, you guys." The others followed her reluctantly, trying hard to look as if they were doing it because they wanted to and not because Buffy had told them to. As she walked away, Jill glanced back at Joanne with a sorrowful expression.

Joanne smiled at her. "Is it okay if I call you?"

Jill smiled, despite the glare Buffy threw at her, and nodded to Joanne. Then she turned away and disappeared around the corner with the others.

As soon as they were gone, the gang whooped and congratulated each other with high fives.

"Well, that's that," Novi said as she closed and locked her locker.

The others did the same. "Mission accomplished," Cam said, taking Novi's hand as they walked towards the exit.

"You were right, Joanne," Leona said, giving Joanne a friendly punch in the arm. "Sorry I ever doubted you."

Joanne smiled shyly and thanked Leona.

"Let's go eat," Horace said. "Something really greasy and awful."

A chorus of agreement followed this suggestion, and the gang danced and jumped through the halls, planning their weekend activities as they went out onto the school parking lot, where they piled into Leona's repaired car. Leona put a tape in the cassette deck and turned up the volume, and they drove away.

Twenty-five

friday march 14

it's been a busy couple of days since i've written in this book. this afternoon was our air guitar triumph. joanne's plan was absolutely brilliant, and obviously effective, because buffy came to our hallway and told us to leave her alone. ah! the tables are turned. i think it's finally finished. thank goodness.

another great thing is joanne. she's so much happier now. and it's nice that she's so different from me. she's a little shy and what I might call uptight, but she makes me think. maybe i don't have to try so hard to show i'm an individual. i mean, joanne has gone from being a part of a gang to being her own person and she still looks the same as she did before. i think she could use some changes, but i could too.

this seems weird to say but i think coming here was meant to be. i mean, my whole family mess is hard and sometimes i just feel so rotten about it all, but in another way i feel better than i've ever felt. cam and joanne and i have been through so much together, i think maybe everything kind of pushed us into getting closer than most people get to each other. and it's like there are whole new areas of life that i've never thought about before and i want to start thinking about them. i need to. sometimes when i talk to joanne or cam about stuff or when i'm with joanne's family i feel, i don't know, true i guess, like the way i feel is the way i'm supposed to feel. in spite of everything, i really feel lucky. but maybe it's not luck i feel. maybe it's love.

Twenty-six

"I'm kind of embarrassed, but this will be my first real date," Novi admitted.

"You're kidding."

"I've gone out before, of course, but, I mean, it was always 'Hey, Nov, wanna go for a burger?' Stuff like that."

"Cam's such a gentleman." Joanne swooned. Novi threw a sock at her.

They were in Novi's room. Novi sat on the floor in front of her mirror putting on her makeup. Joanne stood in front of Novi's closet, occasionally taking articles of clothing out for a closer look.

"What the heck?" Joanne asked, holding up a fringed suede vest.

Novi glared at her cousin. "You are so provincial, Joanne. You wouldn't know cutting edge fashion if it fell on your head."

Joanne hung the vest back in the closet and flopped down on Novi's bed. "I know. I hate it. I've got absolutely no sense of style."

"Well," Novi said, turning to Joanne and looking her over. "You must have some. Somewhere."

"Thank you very much," Joanne sneered. "I could be very sensitive about this. You should be kinder. In fact, I am very sensitive."

"I'm sorry," Novi said. She finished putting on her mascara, then stood up and went to the closet, pulling out a pair of jeans, and an oversized paisley shirt. "Try this."

Novi went back to her makeup while Joanne changed. Joanne got Novi's boots from the closet and put those on too, then stood behind Novi and looked herself over in the mirror.

"I like it." Joanne smiled.

"Try something else on," Novi suggested. "I have to brush my teeth, so that my breath will be fresh and clean for my big date. I'll be right back." Novi lifted her eyebrows diabolically. "Surprise me."

"It's not really about clothes," Joanne yelled to Novi, as she picked out some clothes from the closet.

Novi didn't answer.

"Clothes are kind of beside the point," Joanne decided as she changed her outfit.

"What?" Novi asked, returning from the bathroom.

"I was just thinking that clothes don't really make the man."

"Or the girl," Novi said as she eyed Joanne, who was perched on the bed, decked out in Novi's baggy orange pants, a purple mock turtleneck, and the suede vest.

"Well?" Joanne said, doing a few model turns to give Novi the full view of her outfit.

"Well."

Joanne laughed as she got down off the bed. "What? You don't like it?"

"I don't think it's you, Joanne," Novi said as she began to tease her hair. "I don't think it's anyone, for that matter."

Joanne looked at herself in the mirror. "No, you're right. I don't think this is me. But Novi"—she took Novi by the shoulders and shook her—"what is me?"

"I don't know," Novi said, laughing, and trying to free

herself from her cousin's grasp. "But you'll figure it out eventually."

After Novi left with Cam on their date, Joanne began to feel a little lonely. All her time had been filled with company and plans these past few days, and she hadn't really had to face herself alone yet. She had warded off doubts by keeping busy, but now she was alone and, for the moment, with nothing to do, little insecurities began to creep into her mind. *Does Novi really like me, or does she just feel sorry for me? Maybe I'll never make any other friends. I could be out tonight instead of sitting home alone. Maybe I did the wrong thing.*

As soon as she thought this, though, she realized what was happening. She was just bored, that's all. Just because she wasn't with anyone at this moment didn't mean that no one liked her or that she would always be alone. *But it's reality,* she said to herself, *that there's not always going to be someone around to entertain me.* She stood in her room by her desk aimlessly picking up objects — a book, a note pad, an empty glass — and putting them down again. *There are times when you're by yourself,* she admitted. *This isn't such a terrible thing. I just need to have things to do, stuff that I'm interested in. It's useless to sit around feeling sorry for myself and being bored.*

She walked to her window and looked out at the street. The snow on the front lawn glowed in the street light, and the slick ice on the road shimmered. She pressed her forehead against the cold glass and blew a round cloud of sublimated breath onto the window. She didn't quite know what she wanted to accomplish or learn, what great work she wanted to be excited about and to really throw herself into, but she knew there had to be something. She felt an unfocused but bright hope that she would find something that would make her life more than just empty time to fill, because she really believed life was more than that.

Joanne was still standing with her forehead pressed

against the window when Scott pounded on the door, then burst into the room. Joanne turned around.

"Hey. You're getting better, Scotty. You actually knocked. Thanks." Joanne's voice was only slightly sarcastic.

"Dad said to ask if you wanted to rent a video tonight." Joanne thought for a minute. Not long ago she would have been embarrassed at the idea of spending Saturday night with her family, but as she considered it now it seemed a lot less humiliating than spending more time with her old gang. In fact, it seemed downright appealing.

"Count me in," she said to Scott.

He brightened perceptibly, not having believed before that Joanne would want to spend any time at home with her family. He sped away, yelling as he ran down the stairs, "Hey Dad, she wants to. She wants to."

Joanne couldn't help smiling. Obviously it didn't take much to make her little brother happy. *I never even tried before,* she realized. *As if it would have cost me anything.* A small idea began to form in her mind. She could hear her family in the front hall trying to decide which movie to get. She turned out her light and went downstairs to join them.